D0460969

**HELEN HALL LIBRARY**
City of League City
100 West Walker
League City, TX 77573-3899

JAN    2002

# MOTHER TERESA

# MOTHER TERESA

Tracey E. Dils

**HELEN HALL LIBRARY**
City of League City
100 West Walker
League City, TX 77573-3899

DISCARD

CHELSEA HOUSE PUBLISHERS
PHILADELPHIA

Dedicated to Emily, Phillip, Grace, and Caroline.

*Frontispiece:* Mother Teresa has won international renown and admiration for devoting her life to helping the world's victims of poverty and violence.

PRODUCED BY 21st Century Publishing and Communications, Inc., New York, N.Y.

**Chelsea House Publishers**
EDITOR IN CHIEF Sally Cheney
ASSOCIATE EDITOR IN CHIEF Kim Shinners
PRODUCTION MANAGER Pamela Loos
ART DIRECTOR Sara Davis
DIRECTOR OF PHOTOGRAPHY Judy L. Hasday
COVER ILLUSTRATOR Neilson Carlin
COVER DESIGNER Keith Trego

© 2001 by Chelsea House Publishers, a subsidiary of Haights Cross Communications. All rights reserved. Printed and bound in the United States of America.

The Chelsea House World Wide Web address is
http://www.chelseahouse.com

First Printing
1  3  5  7  9  8  6  4  2

**Library of Congress Cataloging-in-Publication Data**

Dils, Tracey E.
Mother Teresa / Tracey Dils.
    p.   cm.  — (Women of achievement)
Includes bibliographical references and index.
ISBN 0-7910-5887-5 (alk. paper) — ISBN 0-7910-5888-3 (pbk.: alk. paper)
1. Teresa, Mother, 1910 —Juvenile literature.  2. Missionaries of Charity—
Biography—Juvenile literature. [1. Teresa, Mother, 1910– .  2. Missionaries
of Charity.  3. Missionaries.  4. Nuns.  5. Women—Biography.  6. Nobel
Prizes—Biography.]  I. Title. II. Series.

BX4406.5.Z8 D55  2000
271'.97—dc21
[B]                                              00-060155

271.97
D579m

# CONTENTS

# WOMEN of ACHIEVEMENT

**Jane Addams**
SOCIAL WORKER

**Madeleine Albright**
STATESWOMAN

**Marian Anderson**
SINGER

**Susan B. Anthony**
WOMAN SUFFRAGIST

**Clara Barton**
AMERICAN RED CROSS FOUNDER

**Margaret Bourke-White**
PHOTOGRAPHER

**Rachel Carson**
BIOLOGIST AND AUTHOR

**Cher**
SINGER AND ACTRESS

**Hillary Rodham Clinton**
FIRST LADY AND ATTORNEY

**Katie Couric**
JOURNALIST

**Diana, Princess of Wales**
HUMANITARIAN

**Emily Dickinson**
POET

**Elizabeth Dole**
POLITICIAN

**Amelia Earhart**
AVIATOR

**Gloria Estefan**
SINGER

**Jodie Foster**
ACTRESS AND DIRECTOR

**Betty Friedan**
FEMINIST

**Althea Gibson**
TENNIS CHAMPION

**Ruth Bader Ginsburg**
SUPREME COURT JUSTICE

**Helen Hayes**
ACTRESS

**Katharine Hepburn**
ACTRESS

**Mahalia Jackson**
GOSPEL SINGER

**Helen Keller**
HUMANITARIAN

**Ann Landers/
Abigail Van Buren**
COLUMNISTS

**Barbara McClintock**
BIOLOGIST

**Margaret Mead**
ANTHROPOLOGIST

**Edna St. Vincent Millay**
POET

**Julia Morgan**
ARCHITECT

**Toni Morrison**
AUTHOR

**Grandma Moses**
PAINTER

**Lucretia Mott**
WOMAN SUFFRAGIST

**Sandra Day O'Connor**
SUPREME COURT JUSTICE

**Rosie O'Donnell**
ENTERTAINER AND COMEDIAN

**Georgia O'Keeffe**
PAINTER

**Eleanor Roosevelt**
DIPLOMAT AND HUMANITARIAN

**Wilma Rudolph**
CHAMPION ATHLETE

**Elizabeth Cady Stanton**
WOMAN SUFFRAGIST

**Harriet Beecher Stowe**
AUTHOR AND ABOLITIONIST

**Barbra Streisand**
ENTERTAINER

**Elizabeth Taylor**
ACTRESS AND ACTIVIST

**Mother Teresa**
HUMANITARIAN AND
RELIGIOUS LEADER

**Barbara Walters**
JOURNALIST

**Edith Wharton**
AUTHOR

**Phillis Wheatley**
POET

**Oprah Winfrey**
ENTERTAINER

**Babe Didrikson Zaharias**
CHAMPION ATHLETE

# "REMEMBER THE LADIES"

## MATINA S. HORNER

"Remember the Ladies." That is what Abigail Adams wrote to her husband John, then a delegate to the Continental Congress, as the Founding Fathers met in Philadelphia to form a new nation in March of 1776. "Be more generous and favorable to them than your ancestors. Do not put such unlimited power in the hands of the Husbands. If particular care and attention is not paid to the Ladies," Abigail Adams warned, "we are determined to foment a Rebellion, and will not hold ourselves bound by any Laws in which we have no voice, or Representation."

The words of Abigail Adams, one of the earliest American advocates of women's rights, were prophetic. Because when we have not "remembered the ladies," they have, by their words and deeds, reminded us so forcefully of the omission that we cannot fail to remember them. For the history of American women is as interesting and varied as the history of our nation as a whole. American women have played an integral part in founding, settling, and building our country. Some we remember as remarkable women who—against great odds—achieved distinction in the public arena: Anne Hutchinson, who in the 17th century became a charismatic religious leader; Phillis Wheatley, an 18th-century black slave who became a poet; Susan B. Anthony, whose name is synonymous with the 19th-century women's rights movement, and who led the struggle to enfranchise women; and in the 20th century, Amelia Earhart, the first woman to cross the Atlantic Ocean by air.

These extraordinary women certainly merit our admiration, but other women, "common women," many of them all but forgotten, should also be recognized for their contributions to American thought and culture. Women have been community builders; they have founded schools and formed voluntary associations to help those in need; they have assumed the major responsibility for rearing children, passing on from one generation to the next the values that keep a culture alive. These and innumerable other contributions, once ignored, are now being recognized by scholars, students, and the public. It is exciting and gratifying that a part of our history that was hardly acknowledged a few generations ago is now being studied and brought to light.

In recent decades, the field of women's history has grown from obscurity to a politically controversial splinter movement to academic respectability, in many cases mainstreamed into such traditional disciplines as history, economics, and psychology. Scholars of women, both female and male, have organized research centers at such prestigious institutions as Wellesley College, Stanford University, and the University of California. Other notable centers for women's studies are the Center for the American Woman and Politics at the Eagleton Institute of Politics at Rutgers University; the Henry A. Murray Research Center for the Study of Lives, at Radcliffe College; and the Women's Research and Education Institute, the research arm of the Congressional Caucus on Women's Issues. Other scholars and public figures have established archives and libraries, such as the Schlesinger Library on the History of Women in America, at Radcliffe College, and the Sophia Smith Collection, at Smith College, to collect and preserve the written and tangible legacies of women.

From the initial donation of the Women's Rights Collection in 1943, the Schlesinger Library grew to encompass vast collections documenting the manifold accomplishments of American women. Simultaneously, the women's movement in general and the academic discipline of women's studies in particular also began with a narrow definition and gradually expanded their mandate. Early causes, such as woman suffrage and social reform, abolition, and organized labor were joined by newer concerns, such as the history of women in business and the professions and in politics and government; the study of the family; and social issues such as health policy and education.

Women, as historian Arthur M. Schlesinger, jr., once pointed out, "have constituted the most spectacular casualty of traditional history. They have made up at least half the human race, but you could never tell that by looking at the books historians write." The new breed of historians is remedying that omission. They have written books about immigrant women and about working-class women who struggled for survival in cities and about black women who met the challenges of life in rural areas. They are telling the stories of women who, despite the barriers of tradition and economics, became lawyers and doctors and public figures.

The women's studies movement has also led scholars to question traditional interpretations of their respective disciplines. For example, the study of war has traditionally been an exercise in military and political analysis, an examination of strategies planned and executed by men. But scholars of women's history have pointed out that wars have also been periods of tremendous change and even opportunity for women, because the very absence of men on the home front enabled them to expand their educational, economic, and professional activities and to assume leadership in their homes.

The early scholars of women's history showed a unique brand of courage in choosing to investigate new subjects and take new approaches to old ones. Often, like their subjects, they endured criticism and even ostracism by their academic colleagues. But their efforts have unquestionably been worthwhile, because with the publication of each new study and book another piece of the historical patchwork is sewn into place, revealing an increasingly comprehensive picture of the role of women in our rich and varied history.

Such books on groups of women are essential, but books that focus on the lives of individuals are equally indispensable. Biographies can be inspirational, offering their readers the example of people with vision who have looked outside themselves for their goals and have often struggled against great obstacles to achieve them. Marian Anderson, for instance, had to overcome racial bigotry in order to perfect her art and perform as a concert singer. Isadora Duncan defied the rules of classical dance to find true artistic freedom. Jane Addams had to break down society's notions of the proper role for women in order to create new social situations, notably the settlement house. All of these women had to come to terms both with themselves and with the world in which they lived. Only then could they move ahead as pioneers in their chosen callings.

Biography can inspire not only by adulation but also by realism. It helps us to see not only the qualities in others that we hope to emulate, but also, perhaps, the weaknesses that made them "human." By helping us identify with the subject on a more personal level they help us feel that we, too, can achieve such goals. We read about Eleanor Roosevelt, for instance, who occupied a unique and seemingly enviable position as the wife of the president. Yet we can sympathize with her inner dilemma; an inherently shy woman, she had to force herself to live a most public life in order to use her position to benefit others. We may not be able to imagine ourselves having the immense poetic talent of Emily Dickinson, but from her story we can understand the challenges faced by a creative woman who was expected to fulfill many family responsibilities. And though few of us will ever reach the level of athletic accomplishment displayed by Wilma Rudolph or Babe Zaharias, we can still appreciate their spirit, their overwhelming will to excel.

A biography is a multifaceted lens. It is first of all a magnification, the intimate examination of one particular life. But at the same time, it is a wide-angle lens, informing us about the world in which the subject lived. We come away from reading about one life knowing more about the social, political, and economic fabric of the time. It is for this reason, perhaps, that the great New England essayist Ralph Waldo Emerson wrote in 1841, "There is properly no history: only biography." And it is also why biography, and particularly women's biography, will continue to fascinate writers and readers alike.

*Mother Teresa bends to help a destitute woman living on the streets. Her missionary work with the homeless and poor in Calcutta, India, impelled her to establish her first home where those at the end of their lives could die a beautiful death with peace and dignity.*

# 1

# A BEAUTIFUL DEATH

The year was 1952, and the slums of Calcutta, India, teemed with thousands of homeless people. Men, women, and children, many sick or diseased, lived on the streets, often begging for scraps of food. Scores had lived their entire lives on the streets. Many others died on the pavements where they had lived. Those who were strong enough looked for any kind of work to keep from starving.

Moving among the people on a particular day was a tiny woman with a soft face and compassionate eyes. She wore a simple gown, called a sari, with three plain blue stripes and a cross pinned to the left shoulder. Mother Teresa, who would come to be called the "saint of the gutter," was no stranger to Calcutta's poverty. From her convent, she went out day after day to try and ease the misery of the destitute. Along with others from the convent, she passed out food and cared for the sick.

On this day, however, it was not only the hungry and sick who commanded Mother Teresa's attention. Lying on a pile of garbage in the stifling heat, while rats gnawed at her feet, a woman lay dying. For Mother Teresa, dying in the streets, alone and in pain, was the worst kind of indignity. The sight of the suffering woman impelled the energetic nun to immediate action.

With a companion, Mother Teresa gathered up the woman and hurried her to a hospital, where she was turned away. There were only enough beds in the overcrowded hospitals for those who could be cured. Despite being refused, Mother Teresa did not give up. Finally, at one hospital, she simply would not budge until the woman was taken in to lie on a mattress on the floor, where she died a few hours later. Mother Teresa has said "It was then that I decided to find a place for the dying and take care of them myself."

According to some, this incident in the streets of Calcutta has been overdramatized. Whether it is or not, the death of this unknown woman galvanized Mother Teresa. She was going to rescue the dying from the streets and give them final moments of peace and dignity. Relying on little more than her own determination and her belief that God would provide, she took action.

Mother Teresa was not unknown in the slums of Calcutta. In 1950, she had founded her order, the Missionaries of Charity, to serve the city's poor. Now she was going to begin her special work—to provide a haven for those abandoned to die.

Without hesitating, she asked a Calcutta health official, Dr. Ahmad, to find a place in which she could care for those she called "the poorest of the poor." Mother Teresa was very persuasive; she was also adamant about her mission. Although skeptical, Dr. Ahmad agreed to locate a place for her. What he eventually found was an empty building that once housed Hindu pilgrims who worshiped at the nearby temple of the goddess Kali. In the Hindu religion, Kali is the goddess of violence and destruction. A

place symbolizing death would become a refuge for those whose lives were ending.

The building itself was filthy, but Mother Teresa and her sisters faced the challenge. Setting to work, they scrubbed the walls and floors. They scavenged sheets, cots, and mattresses. In less than 24 hours, the building was ready for its peaceful purpose. Mother Teresa promptly named her refuge Nirmal Hriday Home for Dying Destitutes. In Bengali, the language of the state of West Bengal in which Calcutta is located, Nirmal Hriday means "Pure Heart."

Mother Teresa and her sisters searched the streets, looking for those near death. They carried them from

*With the sisters of her missionary order, Mother Teresa sought out those near death in the alleys and streets of Calcutta. Here, Mother Teresa, in front, walks with two young nuns helping a frail, aging man to her Nirmal Hriday Home for Dying Destitutes.*

*The interior of a Hindu temple displays elaborate columns and carvings. The statue is that of a cow, an animal sacred to Hindus.*

## Hindu Religious Beliefs

Brought to India by early invaders, the Hindu religion developed over the centuries into a complex set of beliefs and religious practices. The gods and goddesses of Hinduism are various forms of the one true god, Brahma, with whom Hindus try to unite their lives. Hindus may choose among the many deities a god or goddess who will guide them in following their dharma—ethical duties performed in their worldly lives. Keeping the proper dharma is essential to Hindu beliefs about the afterlife.

For all Hindus, no matter which deity they choose to worship, the center of their religion is the belief in reincarnation, the rebirth of the soul into another body. One who is ethical and has followed his or her dharma will be reborn into a good life. If a person has sinned or neglected his or her dharma, the soul will suffer in a lesser life. The cycle of reincarnation can be repeated over and over again, and few will attain the spiritual perfection to be united with Brahma.

For the dying, Hindus perform rituals that include prayers, readings from sacred texts, and offerings to help the soul on its way to a new body. Because at death only the soul is important as it begins its journey, Hindus regard the body as useless at that point. After death, the body must be taken away as soon as possible and cremated. For those "poorest of the poor" whom Mother Teresa vowed to help, the comfort of receiving Hindu death rituals did not exist.

the streets and alleyways of Calcutta—sometimes by wheelbarrow—to Nirmal Hriday. There they washed them and offered food if the people were able to eat. Providing such simple comforts as holding emaciated hands, stroking shoulders, or just cutting hair brought peace to the dying. In keeping with Mother Teresa's philosophy of respect and tolerance for others' religions, no one was turned away. The dying also received the rituals of their individual faiths. Hindus were touched on the lips with water from the sacred Ganges River; Muslims listened to readings from their sacred book, the Koran.

"When we rescue the dying," Mother Teresa said, "they are scared, distressed, and in despair. But seeing our calm and serene faces bending over them with tenderness and love and listening to our words of faith and hope, they close the door on their lives with a smile on their lips."

Nirmal Hriday faced considerable opposition. Many Hindus were outraged that a place for the dying was so close to the temple of Kali. Others were convinced that Mother Teresa was trying to convert the dying to Christianity. The temple priests were especially incensed. Angry protesters often gathered outside Nirmal Hriday, screaming insults. Some threw sticks and stones at the sisters as they tried to hurry the sick through the doorway. One man even threatened Mother Teresa's life. Others petitioned the city of Calcutta to evict the white-clothed angels of mercy.

The threats and demonstrations brought an inspection by officials. When, however, they saw a clean, orderly place, with sisters caring so willingly and patiently for the people, the officials refused to take action. Opposition also began to diminish when Nirmal Hriday took in a young Hindu priest from the temple of Kali. He was dying of tuberculosis, and no hospital would admit him. Mother Teresa welcomed

*At the Nirmal Hriday home, Mother Teresa saw to the needs of the dying. Their beds were clean mattresses on the floor, and she and the sisters provided food and comfort for those nearing death.*

him and cared for him until he died. The other Kali priests learned that Mother Teresa had the young man cremated according to Hindu rites, and their opposition ceased. Nirmal Hriday was being accepted and would continue to be a peaceful last haven for those facing death.

From its modest beginning in 1952, Nirmal Hriday attracted scores of volunteers to help the sisters in their work. As Mother Teresa's reputation grew, recognition of her work and donations of money and aid enabled her to open homes for the dying in cities across India.

What Mother Teresa provided, she claimed, was more than medical treatment and comfort. What she gave the wounded and dying was a beautiful death. When once asked why it was that the dying at Nirmal Hriday seemed unafraid of death, she quoted the words of one who said: "I've lived like an animal in the street but I will die like an angel." And, Mother Teresa added, "with love and care."

Teenage Agnes Gonxha Bojaxhiu (left), who later became Mother Teresa, poses with her sister, Age. Growing up in a loving family, Agnes was greatly influenced by her mother's strong Roman Catholic faith and by the charity her parents showed toward those less fortunate.

# 2

# WHERE
# CHARITY BEGAN

The woman who became known as Mother Teresa began her life as Agnes Gonxha Bojaxhiu on August 26, 1910, in the town of Skopje in what was then Serbia. Today Skopje is the capital of Macedonia, which is located in southeastern Europe in the region known as the Balkan Peninsula. At the time of Agnes's birth the area was ruled by Turkey, as part of the Ottoman Empire. Many different ethnic groups lived in the Ottoman Empire, including Turks, Greeks, Albanians, Serbs, and Croats. People were also of different faiths: Muslims, followers of Islam, lived alongside Eastern Orthodox and Roman Catholic Christians. Agnes's family was of Albanian descent, and they were Roman Catholics, a minority in Skopje. The majority ethnic group at the time consisted of Serbs, whose religion was Eastern Orthodox. Muslims also lived in Skopje, worshiping in the local mosques.

The third child of the family, Agnes joined her two older siblings—her seven-year-old brother, Lazar, and four-year-old sister, Age. Agnes's father, Nikola Bojaxhiu, was a traveling merchant who was often away from home. Her mother, Dranafile Bernai, took the traditional role of wife and mother, caring for her household and her children. Because of Nikola's business, the family was relatively well-off compared to many others. They lived in a home surrounded by flower gardens and fruit trees on the same street as their church, the Church of the Sacred Heart.

In later years, Mother Teresa was reluctant to reveal too much about her childhood. She believed that her important work was to serve God and that details about her early days were irrelevant. She did reveal to one biographer that her family spent happy times praying together each evening. She also told another biographer of her closeness to her mother and of her mother's influence on her. "She taught us to love God and to love our neighbor," Mother Teresa said. She also noted that the children called Dranafile *Nana Loke*, the "mother of my soul."

Mother Teresa remembered that her mother kept very busy while Nikola worked. When he came home, however, household work stopped. Dranafile donned a clean dress and brushed her hair to greet her husband properly. And she saw to it that the children also welcomed him politely and in clean attire.

Agnes's brother, Lazar, has also given a glimpse into the life of the Bojaxhiu family. In 1979, he recalled that Agnes, who was called Gonxha ("Little Flower"), was a happy child, always willing to help others. She was also a serious child, who, Lazar said, had very strong ideas of obedience to the rules of their church.

Lazar liked to sneak to the kitchen for a snack late at night. Agnes caught him at it and lectured him, reminding him that he could not have any food after midnight if he was to attend mass in the morning. She did not, however, tell their mother about Lazar's late-night forays. And, of course, Agnes herself never raided the kitchen on the night before mass.

Both Nikola and Dranafile were generous to others, and they encouraged their children to do the same.

Borders of the Ottoman Empire in 1912 before the Balkan Wars

/ / / / Territory lost by the Ottoman Empire in the Balkan Wars

When beggars appeared at the door, they never left empty-handed. According to Lazar, Dranafile, accompanied by Agnes, often walked the streets of Skopje, giving food to the hungry. Dranafile was also a significant influence on young Agnes's devotion to God. She was committed to her Catholic faith and took the children to mass every morning. The Church of the Sacred Heart and the small Catholic community in Skopje served as an extended family for the Bojaxhius.

*When Agnes was born in 1910, her birthplace of Skopje was located in part of the Turkish Ottoman Empire. Two years later, as a result of the First Balkan War, the region was freed from Ottoman rule but the area remained a scene of political turmoil.*

*Second from left, Agnes is shown with other students at the School of the Sacred Heart. She was an excellent student and had great musical talent.*

Agnes was probably also influenced by her mother's very practical side. Mother Teresa once revealed an incident from her childhood that reflected her mother's disapproval of wastefulness. One evening the children were chattering away in what their mother considered useless talk. Dranafile simply turned off all the electricity in the house. As Mother Teresa told it, her mother said that "there was no use wasting electricity so that such foolishness could go on."

The family's faith was sorely tested when Nikola died suddenly in 1918 (or 1919 as other records indicate). The records are not clear on the year of his death or on the cause. Nikola had been for many years involved in a political movement to unite all Albanians in one nation. Apparently he was on his way home from a meeting some miles away when he collapsed. Despite efforts to save him, he died. Some said he was poisoned by his political enemies, and apparently the family, especially Lazar, believed that he was. Whatever brought about Nikola's death, he left his widow and children in dire straits. The family business was in shambles, and Dranafile was paralyzed by her grief.

Struggling to recover, Dranafile put her faith in God, and rose above the tragedy. It was essential that she earn a living. With renewed energy, she turned to a skill she knew well—sewing. Soon, Dranafile had begun a small business selling embroidered cloth.

With her father's death, Agnes and her mother drew even closer to each other. They also seemed even more committed to their church and to helping others. They prayed together in church and at home, and they continued being generous to others. The family gave clothing to the needy and often shared its meals with the less fortunate. In later years, Mother Teresa recalled how she helped her mother bathe the wounds of an alcoholic woman. At another time, mother and daughter offered comfort to a woman who was dying and helped care for her children.

According to Mother Teresa, she received her first calling to serve God when she was 12 years old. "I heard the voice of God calling me to be all his, consecrating myself to him and to the service of my neighbors. . . . I was singing in my heart, full of joy inside. It was then that I realized that my vocation was for the poor."  .

Obviously too young to become a nun, Agnes was nevertheless beginning the journey that would lead to her life's work. She threw herself into church activities and was especially musical. The sexton of the Church of the Sacred Heart particularly remembered her. "I knew all the Catholic families," he told an interviewer. "Anges's family was very religious. She herself had a very fine voice; she was really our prima donna, the soprano soloist of the parish choir." He added that Agnes "also directed the choir in the absence of the choirmaster."

In addition to her musical talent, Agnes was a bright student at her secondary school. A cousin remembers that she was an excellent organizer and was reliable and responsible. The teenager enjoyed teaching as well. She often tutored her classmates and taught Albanian children the Catholic faith in their own language. At that time, schoolchildren in Skopje were taught in the Serb language.

Agnes also immersed herself in the activities of a youth organization for girls called the Sodality of the Blessed Virgin Mary. The group had been organized by Father Franjo Jambrenkovic, who came to the Church of the Sacred Heart in 1925. Recognizing her religious fervor, Father Jambrenkovic nutured it.

An avid reader, Agnes pored over works on the lives of the saints and the Catholic missions. She collected money for the poor and prayed for missionaries who had gone to far-off places. She also prayed fervently about the call she believed she had received, hoping it was genuine and that God would eventually reveal his will for her.

Agnes turned to Father Jambrenkovic for advice. When she asked him how she would know whether the call was real, he replied that her own joy in receiving that call would answer the question. "If the thought that God may be calling you to serve him and your neighbor makes you happy, that may be the very best proof of the genuineness of your vocation. Joy that comes from the depths of your being is like a compass by which you can tell that direction your life should follow."

At home, Agnes's siblings were going in their own new directions. Age, who had always been a bright student, left home to enter a commercial college. Lazar had received an academic prize that allowed him to study in Austria. Agnes's path was still uncertain.

When Father Jambrenkovic shared with Agnes and other members of Sodality news of Jesuit missionary work in India, Agnes's future became clearer to her. She listened to the priest's descriptions of dreadful conditions in India—malaria, leprosy, malnutrition, and starvation. She began reading all she could about India in the magazine *Catholic Missions*. The photographs of the sick and the dying especially moved her. As Agnes listened and read, she knew where her future lay. Many years later, she recalled in her simple, direct way: "At eighteen I decided to leave home to become a nun. By then I realized my vocation was towards the poor. From then on, I have never had the least doubt of my decision."

Father Jambrenkovic was not surprised by Agnes's decision. Her mother, however, was shocked and saddened. Being a nun meant a life of sacrifice. As a nun, Agnes would be symbolically married to Christ. She would take vows of poverty, chastity, and obedience. For Dranafile, the hardest part was accepting the fact that Agnes would leave her family. Although terribly distressed, Dranafile finally made peace with Agnes's decision and told her daughter, "Put your Hand in His—in His Hand—and walk all the way with Him."

Age too was saddened, but she realized how important it was for Agnes to follow her heart. Lazar, however, was not as accepting. By then he was a lieutenant in the military service of the new king of Albania. When he wrote Agnes demanding to know how she could do such a thing, she wrote back a simple reply:

"You will serve a king of two million people. I shall serve the king of the whole world."

*Agnes (lower right) shared many happy family times with her brother, Lazar, and her sister, Age. When Agnes told them she was going to become a nun, they were saddened by her decision, knowing she would have to leave them, perhaps forever.*

*At the age of 18, Agnes said good-bye to her family and committed her life to God as a nun of the Sisters of Loreto. She was beginning the journey that would lead her to the slums of Calcutta and her ministry to the poor and unwanted.*

# 3

# THE JOURNEY TO GOD

Eighteen-year-old Agnes had applied to the Sisters of Loreto, a teaching order of nuns that served in the province of Bengal in northeastern India. First, however, she had to stay for a time at the order's abbey in Ireland for some basic training. In September 1928, Agnes said farewell to friends, relatives, and members of Sodality who gathered at the train station to see her off. Accompanied by her mother and sister, she traveled to the city of Zagreb (then in Yugoslavia). From there the young woman would go on alone to Ireland to begin her training.

After spending a few days in Zagreb, Agnes bid a tearful goodbye to her mother and sister. She would never see them again. After the long trip to Rathfarnham, Ireland, Agnes arrived at the Loreto abbey, where she was greeted by a magnificent red brick building behind a barred gate.

Inside the abbey's walls, Agnes took the first step toward becoming a nun. She gave up her street clothes and put on a simple long robe and flowing veil. Agnes would study English and learn about the history of the order, but that was only the beginning. At Loreto, she was a postulant, one who had to spend time on probation before taking the next step to holy orders. When she went to India, she would become a novice for two years, during which time she would learn to follow the strict routine of a religious order. It was only after completing her novitiate that Agnes would take her final vows as a nun.

The legacy of the Loreto order was in keeping with Agnes's beliefs. The Loreto Abbey was founded in 1822 in memory of Mary Ward, a woman born in 1585 to a wealthy English family. After becoming a nun in the order of the Poor Clares, Ward felt God had called her to change the way in which nuns lived and worked.

In Mary Ward's time, nuns were required to live and work inside the walls of their convents. They were kept to a strict schedule of prayer and devotion. Ward was determined to found an order that would allow nuns to leave the convents and work outside to minister to the poor. She also believed that prayer should not interfere with the nuns' work outside the convent. For Mary Ward, it was essential to have "the freedom to refer all to God, seeking and finding Him in all things." And, she called for a woman to be the superior general of the order, rather than a male church official.

Such beliefs were completely radical at the time. Ward's ideas flew in the face of the male domination of the Catholic Church. Although she established several girls' schools outside England, the papacy refused all her demands and would not give her official recognition. At one point, she was even imprisoned in a convent for her audacity. Ward died without achieving her goals, and her work was ignored by church leaders for more than two centuries.

However, some knew of Ward's work, including an English nun named Frances Teresa Ball. Determined to carry on Ward's work, in 1822 Ball established the Loreto Abbey, named to honor the Shrine of Loreto in Italy. The abbey's mission was to teach young girls in India, Australia, and South-African countries that were under British rule at the time. However, there seemed to be a contradiction in the Loreto Abbey's mission. While the primary focus of the order's work was the poor, the schools it established served mostly well-to-do families who wanted a British education for their children.

In 1909 Ward's early work was recognized when Mother Catherine Chambers published an extensive biography of Ward's pioneering efforts. By the early 1950s, the Vatican finally recognized Ward's achievements and gave her the credit she deserved.

*Garbed in plain, black robes, Agnes (left) and another novice arrived in India to begin studying and training to become teachers. Once in India, Agnes saw firsthand the appalling poverty she had only read about.*

This was the order Agnes had joined and through which she would teach in India. In November 1928, after only two months at Loreto Abbey, the young novice boarded the ship for India. The weeks-long journey took Agnes and the other novices through the Mediterranean Sea, the Suez Canal, the Red Sea, and the Indian Ocean. Mother Teresa commented little about her first voyage to India. According to one biographer, however, there was no priest on board, a situation that distressed Agnes and her companions. With no one to say mass, give communion, or hear confessions, the faithful young women made the best of it. They said their rosary prayers, sang Christmas hymns, and created a Nativity scene that showed the birth of Jesus—all on the deck of the ship.

The ship was bound for Calcutta, but it stopped first in the city of Madras, on India's southeast coast. Here, Agnes first witnessed the terrible poverty she had only read about before. In a letter that was published in the *Catholic Missions* magazines, she wrote that she and the others were "shocked to the depths of our beings by [the] indescribable poverty. Many families live in the streets, along the city walls, even in places thronged with people. Day and night they live in the open on mats they have made from large palm leaves—or, often, on the bare ground." Agnes concluded by admonishing those back home to stop complaining of their own troubles. They should, she wrote, "offer up thanks to God for blessing them with such abundance."

In January 1929, Agnes arrived in Calcutta. Though overcome once again by the poverty in the streets, she was thankful to finally begin her work. She wrote about her feelings when the ship docked on India's East coast at the Bay of Bengal: "With a joy which I cannot describe we touched the soil of Bengal for the first time. In the convent church we offered up our thanks to the Redeemer for allowing us to arrive safely at our destination. Pray for us a great deal that we may become good and courageous missionaries."

When Agnes arrived in India, the country was a colony of Great Britain. As early as the 1600s, English merchants had established port towns, including Calcutta, as trading centers. As a small nation, Britain relied on its colonies for many products, and India offered resources such as cotton, rice, and tea. India was also divided into scores of states and provinces, each with its own ruler. Divisions among the various governments had made it easy for Britain to move into India and finally in the 19th century establish its rule over the entire country. The British did allow Indian princes to rule some states but others were under direct control of British authorities. All, however, were ultimately ruled by Great Britain.

A land of tremendous contrast in geography, religion, language, and people, India presented a picture of great wealth and abject poverty. Many Indian princes lived in lavish style in magnificent palaces. Wealthy Indians enjoyed lives of ease and luxury. For the most part, British businessmen and officials also lived well, often isolating themselves from the poor behind the walls of grand estates. Elite Britons and Indians seldom came into contact with the less fortunate, unless they served as household servants or as civil servants in local governments. For the millions of remaining Indians, their lives revolved around their villages in the countryside or in the teeming city streets.

Although Agnes had prepared herself for India's poverty, she still could not believe the living conditions of Calcutta's poor. Thousands managed to survive only by picking through garbage or begging. They washed, ate, and lived in the midst of human and animal waste. Diseases such as smallpox, dysentery, and tuberculosis were rampant. The average life span of a poor Indian was only 30 years.

Unlike Agnes's homeland, India was very hot and humid. Temperatures often reached 100 degrees Fahrenheit or more. During the summer intense rainstorms, known as monsoons, flooded the streets of Calcutta.

Agnes and the other novices did not stay long in Calcutta, however. Their destination was the town of Darjeeling, located approximately 400 miles to the north of Calcutta. Darjeeling was a summer home for wealthy Britons who wanted to escape the heat of Calcutta by escaping to the mountain resort town. They built large summer homes, where they enjoyed garden parties and indulged in a taste for good living.

In this environment, Agnes and her companions would begin their training to become nuns. Agnes's life at the convent was structured and rigorous. She studied the rules of the order, the Scriptures, and theology. She began to learn the Hindi and Bengali languages and continued to improve in speaking English, which she had begun to learn in Ireland. She and the other novices also taught boys and girls from the surrounding area for two hours a day.

*The city of Darjeeling, nestled in the mountains north of Calcutta, was a favorite resort for wealthy Britons. It was also the place where Agnes and other novices studied to take their first vows as sisters of the Order of Loreto.*

For two years, Agnes studied and taught. Finally on May 24, 1931, she fulfilled her dream. Agnes Bojaxhiu took her first vows of obedience, chastity, and poverty as a sister of the Loreto order. During the ceremony, Agnes wore the traditional bridal gown. To symbolize her obedience to God and her "death" to worldly things, she lay for a time facedown on the floor. In honor of Saint Thérèse of the Child Jesus, she chose Teresa as her religious name. The saint for whom Agnes named herself was a French woman who had died at the age of 24 after serving as a Carmelite nun. Saint Thérèse had devoted her short life to serving God and had become the patron saint of missions.

After taking her vows, Agnes, now Sister Teresa, returned to Calcutta to begin her teaching. The Loreto order was well known in India for its high quality of teaching. Well-to-do Indians, both Hindu and Muslim, as well as Britons, sent their children for a Loreto education. Calcutta had several Loreto schools, and

Sister Teresa was posted to the Entally district. The Entally school and the convent lay behind walls in a large compound where Sister Teresa and the others were sheltered from the poverty around them, especially the destitution in the nearby slum of Motijhil. Ironically, in Bengali, Motijhil means "Pearl Lake."

The sisters were restricted to the compound, leaving only for emergencies such as a hospital visit or for an annual spiritual retreat in Darjeeling. If it was necessary to leave the compound for any reason, the sisters never went alone. They were driven in a private car and were accompanied by other sisters.

Sister Teresa's first teaching assignment involved two different schools within the compound. The Entally school taught students from wealthy families who wanted their children to have an "English" education. The other school, St. Mary's, took students from less fortunate families and also many who had been orphaned. Some could pay, others could not, but all were treated equally. Sister Teresa's main subject was geography, but she also taught history and the Catholic catechism.

Sister Teresa also helped care for the personal needs of

*After taking vows as a sister of Loreto at the convent in Calcutta, Agnes (right, back row) posed in the traditional habit of her order. She chose the religious name Sister Teresa, after a French nun later canonized as the patron saint of missions.*

*The heavy doors of the entrance gate to the Entally school and convent in Calcutta were usually closed. Until 1935, when she was allowed to teach in a school outside the convent walls, Sister Teresa, as well as her fellow nuns, could seldom venture outside the protected compound.*

girls at St. Mary's, most of whom boarded there. Many years later, Sister Francesca, who had been a pupil of Sister Teresa's, recalled how her teacher had stressed personal cleanliness. Sister Francesca explained that after gathering the girls for their baths, Sister Teresa "would stand there, ring the bell for us to pour water on ourselves, ring the bell for us to soap ourselves, ring the bell for us to pour water again, ring the bell for us to come out."

Like all of the sisters at Loreto, Sister Teresa followed a grueling schedule. After rising before dawn, she said her prayers and then spent the day teaching and supervising the students. She studied to improve her Hindi and Bengali. The evening included more prayers and religious lessons.

In spite of her busy schedule, Sister Teresa found

time to write to her mother and sister and to the *Catholic Missions* magazine. Dranafile and Age had left Skopje and moved with Lazar to the city of Tirana, in Albania. Political turmoil continued to plague the Balkan region, and Sister Teresa no doubt worried about her family.

Although many of the students at St. Mary's school were poor, they did not suffer the degradation of the destitute on the streets. In 1935, Sister Teresa was allowed to teach outside the compound at St. Teresa's, a school that served some of Calcutta's poorest children. Walking the few blocks to St. Teresa's, she saw on a daily basis the poverty that surrounded the convent. She was also shocked by the condition of the school, and as her first task, she cleaned the classroom. Many of the children didn't know what to make of a schoolteacher doing such a menial task. Of the experience, Mother Teresa later wrote in her journal, "I rolled up my sleeves immediately, rearranged the whole room, found water and a broom, and began to sweep the floor. This greatly astonished them. They had never seen a schoolmistress start lessons like that, particularly because in India, cleaning is something that the lower [classes] do."

Soon the children joined in. The girls helped Sister Teresa, and the boys brought water. The classroom became a symbol of the students' pride, and their teacher an inspiration for them. Sister Teresa's reputation as a kind, loving, but no-nonsense teacher spread, and enrollment at the school doubled. The students came to call her "Ma," short for mother. To them, she seemed to be a second mother.

In 1937, Sister Teresa took her final vows, dedicating herself to God's service for the rest of her life. Shortly thereafter, she was named principal of St. Mary's School. Once again, she was enclosed within the compound walls. But having witnessed firsthand the desperate poverty people endured, she encouraged others to venture into the streets. St. Mary's had established a Sodality group like that young Agnes had belonged to in Skopje. Sister Teresa asked some of the older girls at the school to visit the poor in their homes or those in the hospital.

"[Sister Teresa] asked us to gather them around us, teach them the alphabet and some songs, and to make them happy," one of the Sodality members, Subhashini Das, has said.

The lives of the sisters and students in the convent followed a peaceful and orderly pattern. Outside, however, a storm was brewing. In the 1930s, tension and conflict between Indians and the British was escalating with the growing movement for Indian independence. Its leader was Mohandis K. Gandhi, called Mahatma ("Great Soul"). For several years, using nonviolent protest and passive resistance as his weapons, Gandhi and the thousands who followed his movement had struggled for freedom. They were steadily breaking down the walls of British rule. By 1939, it seemed as if the independence movement could not be stopped.

That same year, Nazi Germany began its conquest of Europe, starting World War II (1939–1945). Great Britain was a prime target, and British colonies, including India, were expected to contribute to the war effort with soldiers and supplies. Gandhi refused to cooperate and was jailed, and most Indians objected to becoming involved.

When Japan entered the war in 1941, its proximity to India threatened the colony and the British living there. As a consequence, Indian men by the thousands had to join British forces fighting in Southeast Asia. Great Britain also requisitioned food and supplies from India. For a time, Gandhi's independence movement was stalled.

As the British fought the Japanese in nearby Burma and the colony of Singapore, refugees and wounded soldiers began flooding into Calcutta. The Loreto compound was taken over as a hospital for British soldiers,

## The Caste System

Like the Hindu religion, the caste system of placing people in different social classes came to India with the early invaders. Early Hindu books describe four main castes. Brahmans, the priests and scholars, were at the top. Beneath them were the rulers and warriors, followed by merchants, traders, and farmers. The lowest caste included artisans, laborers, servants, and slaves. Over time, a fifth group was placed outside the caste system—the outcasts, or untouchables. They had the lowly jobs, such as picking up garbage, cleaning toilets, and handling the dead. Members of the other castes believed they would be polluted by any contact with the untouchables.

The system determined a person's place in the society and his or her occupation, and movement from one caste to another was unthinkable. A farmer remained a farmer, and his son would be a farmer. Complex rules governed relationships among the castes. Members of one caste could not eat with those of another caste; marriage outside one's caste would be punished.

In modern India, the caste system is weakening as the nation becomes more urbanized and industrialized. Members of various castes have to work together and mingle in public, especially in the cities. Many rules against personal contact have been relaxed, and discrimination against untouchables, whom Gandhi called harijan, "children of God," is outlawed. The government has also given harijan special employment and educational opportunities, and many have attained high positions. In 1995, for instance, an untouchable woman lawyer who had served in the Indian legislature became the chief minister of the state of Uttar Pradesh. The caste system has not been eradicated, however. In rural areas and in thousands of villages, it remains a strong social force.

and most of its students were sent to convents in and around Calcutta. As the war intensified, Bengal began to face famine. A flood and cyclone destroyed much of the rice crop, Bengal's major food source. What little was left was commandeered by the government to feed Indian and British troops.

Although the Catholic Church and various charities stepped in to try to feed the destitute, the situation soon turned into tragedy for the Bengali people. Figures are not exact, but it is estimated that as many as five million people died of starvation. Sister Teresa and the others in the convent were spared much of the suffering. They taught the remaining students, prayed, and sustained

*A train winds its way through the mountains to Darjeeling. It was on the Darjeeling train that Sister Teresa received the call from God to leave her convent and live among and serve the poorest of the poor.*

themselves on food provided by the Church.

When the war ended in 1945, conditions in India had worsened. Gandhi had been released from jail in 1944, and as the war was coming to a close, he began negotiating with the British for independence. Despite Gandhi's influence and his steadfast principles of nonviolence, bitter conflict broke out between Hindus and Muslims. Each group wanted control of a new government. When it seemed that no compromise could be reached, riots and violence erupted in cities throughout India.

Calcutta was not spared. Mobs of Hindus and Muslims rampaged through the streets. Thousands were killed or wounded; thousands more were driven from their homes. Although Sister Teresa and her companions had had enough food during the war, now supplies were blocked. Desperate for food, Sister Teresa took to the streets. She knew of the riots because the sisters had helped both Hindus and Muslims who had sought refuge in the convent. But she had not seen what was happening outside the walls.

She later told a biographer what she saw there: "We were not supposed to go out into the streets, but I went anyway. Then I saw the bodies on the streets, stabbed, beaten, lying there in strange positions in their dried blood." She continued to describe what happened, telling how she met a group of soldiers who gave her bags of rice and took her back to the compound. These same soldiers and others finally quelled what Bengalis called the Great Killing. The city was in a shambles, and Sister Teresa was filled with sadness at the death and destruction.

Shortly after this experience Sister Teresa became ill, most probably from tuberculosis. In the fall of 1946, despite her condition and the unrest around her, she took the train through the mountains to Darjeeling for her annual spiritual retreat. While on the train she experienced a revelation that changed her life—she heard the voice of God calling her to a new mission. As she later explained:

> I was going to Darjeeling to make my retreat. It was on that train that I heard the call to give up all and follow Him into the slums—to serve Him in the poorest of the poor. I knew it was his will and that I had to follow Him. . . . The message was quite clear. I was to leave the convent and work with the poor while living among them. It was an order. I knew where I belonged, but I did not know how to get there.

That order would change not only Sister Teresa's life but the lives of millions of others.

*Obeying God's call, Sister Teresa left the Loreto order so she could serve the poor. Donning a simple sari, the traditional garb of Indian women, she founded her own order, the Missionaries of Charity.*

# 4

# THE CALL
# TO THE POOR

or Sister Teresa, acting on her divine call would be a wrenching decision. She knew that to serve the poor of the streets, she would have to break her commitment of spending her life teaching in the Loreto order. Her work would also be outside the convent walls, and such an undertaking was expressly forbidden as a nun.

Although convinced of her "call within a call," Sister Teresa did consult her spiritual advisers. Among them was Father Celeste van Exem, a Jesuit priest who had arrived in Calcutta during the war. According to Father van Exem, Sister Teresa wrote down for him her experience, describing how the call came on the train to Darjeeling and how it continued during her retreat.

Father van Exem was convinced of her sincerity, but he could not imagine this frail nun surviving on the streets of Calcutta. He suggested that she write directly to the Vatican for permission to leave the order, or that she contact the Roman Catholic archbishop of Calcutta to ask for his help. Sister Teresa took the second suggestion. Whichever step she took, however, her request would in the end have to be approved by the Loreto Abbey in Ireland, as well as by Pope Pius XII, the head of the Catholic Church in Rome.

Obtaining permission to leave the Loreto order was a lengthy process. Meanwhile Sister Teresa waited patiently in the Asanol convent northwest of Calcutta, to which her order had sent her. There, she wrote letters to Father van Exem and the archbishop of Calcutta. The archbishop was reluctant to allow any nun to move outside her convent and into the streets. After consulting with Father van Exem and other Jesuits, the archbishop finally agreed that as a first step, Sister Teresa could write to the head of the Loreto order in Ireland.

As Sister Teresa waited, the turmoil in India grew. India did become a free nation in 1947, but the cost was great. Because Hindus and Muslims could not agree on who would control the government, the only solution seemed to be the partition of India into two separate nations. India would be Hindu, and Muslims would have the new nation of Pakistan, carved from parts of northern India.

The partition, however, brought more suffering. Hindus living in Muslim-controlled areas fled into Hindu regions. Muslims, who feared the Hindu-run government, sought safety in Muslim regions. The disruption brought more violence, and hundreds of thousands of Hindus and Muslims died. Although Gandhi tried to stem the madness by traveling to areas in conflict with his message of nonviolence, he was unsuccessful. In January 1948, the man who led India to freedom was assassinated by a Hindu fanatic who opposed making peace with Muslims.

In the midst of the turmoil, Sister Teresa received the news she had been praying for. The head of the Loreto order believed that Sister Teresa's calling was from God, and she supported her request. The archbishop of Calcutta finally gave in, and Sister Teresa

wrote to the pope in Rome. In August 1948, almost two years after her revelation ordering her to work with the poor, Sister Teresa was granted permission to serve outside the convent as a Loreto nun. After a year's probationary period, the church leaders would decide whether she could continue her work.

On that August day, Sister Teresa gave up the nun's habit she had worn for 21 years. She put on a white sari, the traditional dress of Indian women, which she had fashioned herself out of the cheapest material she could find. The blue borders she attached were symbolic of the Virgin Mary. With her new habit and a cross pinned to her left shoulder, Sister Teresa left the convent with a small amount of money from her Loreto sisters.

Since she would be ministering to the sick, Sister

*In July 1946, a year before India won its independence from Britain, Mahandas K. Gandhi (right) conferred with India's future prime minister, Jawaharlal Nehru. Both men had fought to free India. In 1948, shortly after India had gained its freedom, Gandhi was assassinated.*

Teresa needed some basic medical skills. She had already written to the mother superior of the Medical Mission Sisters in the city of Patna, north of Calcutta. In describing Sister Teresa's stay at Patna, the nun who directed the mission's nursing school remembered years later: "[Sister] Teresa visited and lovingly attended patients in the wards. As she had never had any nursing before . . . I was able to teach her many simple procedures, making a hospital bed, giving injections and medicines." The sister recalled that Sister Teresa also assisted at births.

Sister Teresa took the practical advice of the nurse-sisters at Patna. Previously she had decided that she and those she recruited to her cause should eat as the poor did— just some rice and salt. The sisters talked her out of that idea. They pointed out that if she was to work in the slums, she needed good nutrition. They also emphasized the importance of rest and personal cleanliness to help avoid the diseases so rampant among the people of the streets. Sister Teresa agreed that she would follow this advice so that she could serve God to the fullest.

After a few weeks, Sister Teresa left Patna and returned to Calcutta to begin her ministry in earnest. She moved into Saint Joseph's House with the Little Sisters of the Poor, an order that served the elderly and the ill. In late December 1948, Sister Teresa entered the streets, walking directly to the Motijhil slum.

Conditions had worsened in Calcutta. Hindu refugees and others torn from their homes crowded every corner of Motijhil. Food and clean water were scarce. As she traveled through the streets, Sister Teresa barely knew where to begin. It seemed that hundreds and hundreds needed her help. She often returned to Saint Joseph's weary and worn and disheartened by what she had seen. At one point, she wrote in her journal: "Oh, God! If I cannot help these

people in their poverty and their suffering, let me at least die with them, close to them so that in that way I can show them your love."

Still, despite her feelings, she remained steadfast in her belief that God would lead her on the right path. That path seemed to be revealed to her when she returned to her first profession—teaching. Gathering the children of Motijhil around her, she began teaching them the Bengali alphabet. Lessons were conducted outside where she drew the letters in the sand with a stick. Soon a regular group of students from

*For thousands of the destitute, the littered streets were their only homes when Sister Teresa began her work in the slums of Calcutta. Although sometimes disheartened by the terrible poverty, she never doubted that God would direct her path.*

the slums looked forward to seeing her each day. In keeping with her ideas of hygiene, Sister Teresa also gave lessons in basic cleanliness by giving bars of soap as rewards for academic progress and good behavior. After school, she often visited her students' homes, teaching their families basic hygiene as well.

But not everyone in Motijhil was glad to see Sister Teresa teaching the children. Some distrusted this strange European woman who made her rounds through the slums. They suspected she had a secret agenda—to convert the people from Hinduism to Christianity. At one point, religious zealots pelted her with stones. Even a Jesuit priest found it hard to understand what impelled her to roam through the filthy alleys and streets. He remarked that he and some others thought she was crazy.

Although Sister Teresa did not waiver from her mission, she did admit to missing her more comfortable life at Loreto. In her journal, she wrote:

> Today I learned a good lesson. The poverty of the poor must be so hard for them. While looking for a home I walked and walked till my arms and legs ached. I thought how much they must ache in body and soul, looking for a home, food and health. Then the comfort of Loreto came to tempt me.

Occasionally, too, she fought back tears, feeling that they were a sign of weakness.

While Sister Teresa was grateful for the hospitality of the Little Sisters of the Poor, she needed a place of her own to carry on her mission. Again, Father van Exem stepped in to help. He contacted a Bengali Christian man, Michael Gomes, who had a large, half-empty house. Gomes let Sister Teresa stay in one of the rooms rent free, and she moved in with a helper, an Indian widow named Charur Ma. Although Michael Gomes offered her furniture, Sister Teresa remained true to her vows of poverty and insisted on simple items—a bed and a wooden crate as an altar.

After establishing a place of her own, Sister Teresa soon found a little hut, which she could use as a school for the children. She rented it with some donation money. As other donations came in, she was able to buy supplies for the school. Small donations were not enough, however. Sister Teresa needed medicines to give to the poor, and she did not hesitate to ask for them. On what she called her "begging trips," she visited pharmacies and asked for donations. According to one story, when she met a pharmacist who refused to help, Sister Teresa simply sat down and said her rosary (a series of prayers) until the exasperated man gave in.

While Sister Teresa continued to visit the slums, often accompanied by Michael Gomes's young daughter, Mabel, she began to gain a reputation among district officials and well-to-do citizens for her compassion, her determination, and her persistence. As her reputation grew, so did donations to her cause. She also gathered around her the first of her volunteers. Young women, many of whom were students from her teaching days at St. Mary's and who were eager to follow in her footsteps, were arriving at the Gomeses' front door.

As the numbers increased, Sister Teresa needed more room, and Gomes offered the third floor of his home. Within the home, the young women followed a strict schedule. Sister Teresa rang a bell each morning at 4:30 to wake them up for prayers, followed by mass. The rest of the morning the young women went into the streets to minister to the poor. After a short lunch break and nap, they returned to their work. At the end of the day they returned home, where they ate dinner, prayed, and went to bed at 10 o'clock.

Sister Teresa's probationary period ended in 1950. Out of her devotion to the people of India, she became an Indian citizen that year. She also set in motion her plans to form her own religious order. First she had to draft a constitution, explaining the rules of the order and its purpose. After explaining her "call within a call," Sister Teresa added the traditional vows of poverty, chastity, and obedience. But she added a fourth vow, which told in simple words the purpose of the order— "to give wholehearted and free service to the poorest of the poor." She also decided on the name of her order: the Missionaries of Charity.

Father van Exem stepped forward once again and supported her request, which went to the archbishop of Calcutta. From there the constitution was sent to Rome for final acceptance from Pope Pius XII. Subashini Das, who had been a Sodality member at St. Mary's School and who eventually took the name Sister Agnes in honor of Sister Teresa's first name, later recalled the waiting: "We felt our way would be recognized, maybe soon, maybe not so soon. But it would happen."

In October 1950, it did happen. At 40 years old, Sister Teresa was confirmed as Mother Teresa, the mother superior of a new order, the Missionaries of Charity. Mother Teresa claimed that the name was directly inspired by God: "It came from the call. It is what we are meant to be: carriers of God's love."

At a special mass to celebrate, Mother Teresa's young volunteers officially became novices. They took the traditional vows of poverty, chastity, and obedience, and the fourth vow to serve the poor. Like the poor, they would have few worldly goods. They would give up all personal income, possessions, and contact with their former lives. Their only clothing would be simple white saris with the distinctive blue stripes, coarse underwear, and open sandals. They would have a rosary, an umbrella, and a bucket for washing. Thin mattresses on the floor would serve as beds. Novices were not permitted to ask for anything for themselves— not even a glass of water or a cup of tea. Everything they requested had to be requested in the name of charity.

Despite the hardships, young women continued to

*After her confirmation as the head of the Missionaries of Charity, Mother Teresa continued to work personally among the poor. With her white robe and her bag tucked under her arm, she was a familiar sight on the streets of Calcutta to both children and adults.*

join Mother Teresa's order. It was not too long before the group had grown too large for the third floor of the Gomeses' home. The sisters needed a building or a house from which to carry on their work. However, Mother Teresa was not discouraged. According to one biographer, "She and her sisters simply added this latest need to their prayers and carried on as before." In her journal Mother Teresa wrote that they "stormed heaven" with their prayers.

Their prayers were answered. According to Sister Agnes, a mysterious man showed up one day and said

*Mother Teresa (seated) prays with the sisters of her order. She set up a rigorous schedule for everyone. In addition to their long hours among the poor in the streets, she and the sisters attended mass in the morning and held prayers in the morning and evening.*

he knew of a three-story building that was available. After leading Mother Teresa to the house, he introduced her to the owner and then disappeared. The owner was astounded. He was planning to sell the place but had told only his wife. Without even bargaining, he agreed to sell the house to the Missionaries of Charity for a fraction of what it was worth.

At their new quarters, the sisters led the same frugal life as before. The rooms were sparsely furnished, and modern conveniences such as stoves, washing machines, and telephones did not exist. The women were expected to cook over a charcoal fire and to endure the intense heat without cooling fans. To serve the poor, Mother Teresa believed that she and the sisters had to live like the poor. Mother Teresa was practical as well. For instance, she calculated that the cost of a telephone could feed scores of Calcutta's destitute. Reluctantly, when she realized that a phone was necessary to help with her mission, she allowed a single phone to be installed.

The women also followed the same strict schedule as before, rising around dawn, working with the poor during the day, and ending their work at 10 P.M. As the order grew and expanded, all Missionaries of Charity would follow the same routine. The Calcutta order's work involved running a soup kitchen as well as walking or riding a streetcar into the sprawling slums, giving out food and medicine and talking to the people about preventing further disease through cleanliness.

Mother Teresa was confident that if she and her sisters continued their hands-on work with the poor, donations would eventually come her way. She continued her begging trips, but refused to mount an organized fund-raising effort or to allow others to raise funds for her. She also refused donations from the Catholic Church or from the Indian government. Instead, she relied on her own power of persuasion, appealing to the consciences of potential donors. She was so effective that donors often gave more than they had intended. Mother Teresa convinced them that their aid would go directly to the poor.

Mother Teresa's 1952 encounter with the woman dying in the streets had inspired the founding of Nirmal Hriday. As a teacher, however, children had always been of special concern to her. After establishing the home for the dying, she turned to the orphans in the slums. In 1955, she opened Shishu Bhavan (Children's Home) to care for abandoned children whose parents had left them rather than face the terrible prospect of watching them starve to death. Other children, including infants, who were disabled or born with defects also found a refuge in the home.

Soon Mother Teresa began opening the home to abandoned or orphaned teenage girls. For these young girls, life on the streets was especially dangerous. They faced possible assault and rape. Some were forced to become prostitutes to earn a meager living. At Shishu Bhavan, they found a safe haven. The sisters also taught them useful skills such as sewing and typing. If they chose to leave the walls of Shishu Bhavan and marry, Mother Teresa always made sure they had a small dowry (money or goods a woman brings to her husband in marriage) to take with them.

Not everyone praised Mother Teresa's work with children and young women, however. Some felt the same resources should be used to encourage family planning or teach birth control. Still others criticized Mother Teresa's firm opposition to abortion. They argued that opposition to family planning, birth control, and abortion contributed to the explosion of India's population and the terrible overcrowding in the cities.

Mother Teresa answered her critics by holding steadfastly to her convictions and official Catholic doctrine. She publicly opposed abortion and birth control under any circumstances. Even abandoning a child was better than killing it, she said. She told this story to demonstrate her beliefs:

> The other day, I picked up a bundle from the street. It looked like a bundle of clothes that somebody had left there, but it was a child. Then I looked: legs, hands, everything was crippled. No wonder someone had left it like that. But how can a mother who did that face God? But one thing I can tell you; the mother—a poor woman—left the child like that, but she did not kill the child, and this is something that we have to learn from our women, the love for the child.

It seemed that Mother Teresa was never fully satisfied with her mission to serve the poor. In 1957 she turned her attention to the lepers of Calcutta. Leprosy is a chronic disease most often, but not always, found in countries with hot climates. It is caused by a bacteria that attacks the skin and nerve endings, slowly destroying muscle and tissue, causing dreadful deformities. Often, as the body deteriorates, infection and gangrene (death of soft tissues due to a loss of blood supply) set in.

Leprosy is also a disease that since ancient times has been widely misunderstood. Although it is contagious, leprosy is not easily spread by casual contact. However, because people have feared contracting the disease, lepers have throughout history been shunned by society and forced to live in isolation. In biblical times, and even later, lepers were forced to carry a bell and ring it to announce their approach. In 20th-century India,

*Mother Teresa blesses orphans at the Children's Home in Calcutta, which she had founded in 1955. Children were always of concern to Mother Teresa, especially those who had been abandoned in the streets. Eventually she founded homes across India that cared for thousands of unwanted children.*

leprosy was still a dreaded disease and still shrouded in mystery. In Calcutta in the late 1950s, some 30,000 lepers lived in shacks in the slums, spurned by their families and by society.

Mother Teresa knew from her medical training that leprosy, if caught early, could be effectively treated and, sometimes, even cured. She also knew that certain medicines and a healthy diet could help more advanced cases. It was essential to teach the sisters to spot the early signs of leprosy so that they could recommend early treatment.

Since Mother Teresa could not allow lepers to be treated at Nirmal Hriday, she needed a way to get to them. "I need a mobile clinic," she told a visitor, "to carry help to the poorest of our poor, the ones who cannot get to the hospital at all." With the help of a donor, she bought a van and had it converted into a treatment facility on wheels. Driving to places around the city, the sisters offered medicine and food. By this time, doctors were also assisting Mother Teresa, and with their help, she set up clinics for women and children in poor areas around Calcutta.

However, Mother Teresa didn't stop there. She actively worked to dispel superstitions that surrounded the disease, establishing a Leprosy Fund and a Leprosy Day, during which she encouraged people to "touch a leper with your compassion." She was also firm in her view that lepers should learn to be self-sufficient. At the clinics, sisters and volunteers taught leprosy victims to weave their own bandages and make their own shoes. They wove fabrics and created simple bags. Mother Teresa carried one of these bags wherever she traveled. Eventually, she established Shanti Nagar, "town of peace," a community for lepers located outside of Calcutta. There, lepers could live with their families and be trained to work in order to support themselves.

Word of Mother Teresa's commitment to caring for lepers, the dying, children, and young women was spreading. Indian newspapers routinely printed articles about this dedicated nun and her Missionaries of Charity. With every article, her support grew. Not only was she receiving the donations she needed to expand her operations, she was receiving hands-on help from volunteers, many of them wealthy people.

Mother Teresa's mission had begun with a simple walk through the slums. In the years since she had taken that walk, she had become an institution.

*A committed and determined Mother Teresa was not content to serve the poor only in Calcutta. After prayer and persistence, she persuaded Catholic churchmen to let her expand her mission throughout India and finally reach beyond to millions of the needy worldwide.*

# 5

# INDIA AND BEYOND

Mother Teresa had begun her religious life cloistered inside the walls of a convent. Her calling had eventually taken her into the streets of Calcutta. But she was not content to stop there. She was aware that suffering and loneliness were everywhere. In 1960, having just turned 50 years old, she gathered her energies to spread the work of her order to those who needed it anywhere in the world.

The first steps were taken inside India. After developing a relationship with bishops in several regions in India, Mother Teresa waited for invitations from the churchmen to establish a mission in their communities. Before she would open a new mission, she insisted that the bishops agree to her conditions. First, the sisters would have to go among the poorest of the poor. Second, they would not be allowed to work to exhaustion so that they had no time for prayer. Finally, a priest had to be available to say mass and to act as a spiritual adviser. If these conditions were met, five or six sisters would then pack up their meager belongings and leave the main quarters in Calcutta to establish a new mission.

*A persuasive speaker for her ministry, Mother Teresa visited the United States and Europe pleading her cause. Although she firmly believed her work was not a business, her staunch commitment to the poor inspired people to donate funds and volunteer their help.*

Mother Teresa's persistence was rewarded. She opened her first mission in Ranchi, a city in the rugged, mountainous region of northeast India. Three other missions followed—in Delhi, Jhansi, and Agra. The opening of the mission in Delhi was attended by India's prime minister Jawaharlal Nehru. Mother Teresa later recalled that when she asked the prime minister if she could tell him about her work, he replied, "No, Mother, you need not tell me about your work. I know about it. That is why I have come."

To expand in the way Mother Teresa planned, her

order would need more funds. Once content to rely on her begging trips to raise money, Mother Teresa now became more assertive. She continued to rely on her belief that God would provide, saying, "I don't want the work to become a business but to remain a work of love. I want you to have that complete confidence that God won't let us down. Take Him at His word and seek first the kingdom of heaven, and all else will be added on. Joy, peace, and unity are more important than money." At the same time, however, she scheduled a trip to the United States in 1960 to spread the word about her mission.

Mother Teresa began her U.S. tour in Las Vegas, Nevada, where she addressed the National Council for Catholic Women. Her work was well known among Catholics in the United States. She had appeared on the cover of the American Catholic magazine *Jubilee*, but she had not yet spoken in public about her mission. Though unpolished in her presentation, Mother Teresa turned out to be a natural crusader for her cause. Without notes, she told her emotional and sometimes harrowing stories of the poverty and sickness on the streets of Calcutta. Though she often spoke in broken English and with incorrect grammar, she always made the mission of her order clear. "We Missionaries of Charity depend on the providence of God," she told listeners. "We don't beg. All we say to Hindus and Muslims and Christians is 'Do something beautiful for God.'"

From Las Vegas, Mother Teresa journeyed to New York City, where she addressed officials of the Catholic Church as well as civic leaders. She also spent time at the United Nations, attempting to raise awareness of the conditions of the poor all over the world.

Throughout her trip, Mother Teresa remained humble, describing herself as merely a vehicle for God's work. "I am like a little pencil in God's hand. He does the thinking. He does the writing. The pencil has only to be allowed to be used."

Wherever she spoke, listeners responded with donations and offers of help. The press responded too, plastering her image in newspapers and magazines, and printing inspirational stories about the Missionaries of Charity. Mother Teresa was uncomfortable in front of cameras and shied away from such publicity. When she discovered how much it could help her cause, however, she justified photo opportunities by praying that God would release one soul from purgatory each time her picture was taken.

From the United States, Mother Teresa traveled to England and Germany, where her speeches continued to inspire press coverage and donations. Her next stop was Rome. There she had a more important goal in mind: to convince Pope John XXIII to place the Missionaries of Charity directly under his leadership instead of that of the archbishop of Calcutta. This change would allow Mother Teresa to expand her mission beyond the borders of India and throughout the world.

However, the pope could not be convinced. Mother Teresa's disappointment over his decision was softened by a tearful reunion with her brother, Lazar, who was living in Italy with his wife, Maria, and their 10-year-old daughter. Brother and sister had not seen each other in 30 years. Dranafile and Age were absent from the family gathering. They were still living in Tirana, Albania, at the time controlled by a Communist government, and were not permitted to leave. Mother Teresa had requested permission several times to enter Albania herself to see them, but her requests were always refused. Communist Albania had banned religion in any form and had closed churches and imprisoned many of the Catholic clergy. There was no doubt that the government considered the presence of a religious figure like Mother Teresa in Albania a threat to its stability.

Once again back in India, Mother Teresa continued to establish foundations for the poor. During the 1960s, the Missionaries of Charity opened several new orphanages and homes in India for the dying, and her work

continued to receive international attention. She too was becoming well known as the recipient of awards. In 1962, on the recommendation of Prime Minister Nehru, she received the Padma Shri ("Magnificent Lotus") Award for public service, an honor never before given to someone not born in India.

The respect and admiration she had earned was evident when she appeared to accept the award. One observer described the scene: "She received the award as she would have received a dying man or picked up a child, but the hall went mad. The stamping and the clapping and the

*Mother Teresa's work was attracting international attention as she expanded her ministry in India. The poor crowded the many centers like this one run by the Missionaries of Charity, which distributed food to those in need.*

cheering were absolutely spontaneous. I looked at the President [of India], there were tears in his eyes."

Later that year, Mother Teresa traveled to the Philippines to receive the Magsaysay Award for International Understanding, given in honor of the late Philippine president. Included with the award was cash. Characteristically, Mother Teresa built a children's home with the funds.

In 1963 Mother Teresa began pursuing an idea she had thought about for some time—to establish a missionary brotherhood. Some tasks, she believed, were simply better suited to men than to women. She received approval from the archbishop of Calcutta to establish the Missionary Brothers of Charity. The word was spread and three young men came forward. Their main purpose was to minister to homeless boys and share the poverty of the poor.

The young men trained under the spiritual guidance of priests in Calcutta and received some medical training. Because a woman could not direct a brotherhood, however, a full-time priest and director was needed. An Australian Jesuit, Father Ian Travers-Ball, soon joined the little group living on one floor of Shishu Bhavan. Taking the name Brother Andrew, he established a separate headquarters for the brotherhood. Under Brother Andrew's leadership, the brothers began working cooperatively but independently of Mother Teresa and the Missionaries of Charity.

Mother Teresa was also eager to expand her mission to other nations. Her prayers were finally answered in 1965, on the 15th anniversary of her order. Pope Paul VI finally placed the Missionaries of Charity directly under his control, and he also agreed that Mother Teresa could expand her order outside India. Once the permission was given, the Missionaries of Charity grew rapidly. The first international home was established in Cocorote, Venezuela, where the sisters set up housekeeping in an old, abandoned hotel. After cleaning the building and

*Once Mother Teresa had received permission to expand her work beyond India, she was a tireless traveler to numerous countries. She founded and visited homes for the poor, sick, and dying, as well as orphanages like this one in Haiti, where she walks with one of the children.*

ridding it of snakes, the sisters began their work—caring for the needs of the town's poor. Expansion to other South American countries soon followed.

In 1966 Mother Teresa returned to Rome, this time to meet with Albanian officials. She hoped she could convince them to allow Dranafile and Age to leave the Communist country. Although the Albanian officials claimed that they were investigating the matter, it was not to happen. Mother Teresa left Rome not knowing whether she would ever lay eyes on her mother and sister again.

Two years later, Mother Teresa traveled to Rome once again, this time with a group of sisters. To her surprise, Pope Paul VI asked that she establish a mission in the city. At first she was reluctant. Dozens of orders lived and worked in Rome. What possible help could the Missionaries of Charity be? However, once Mother Teresa saw the poverty in Rome's outlying areas, she realized the need and knew she had to help the city's poor. Rome's sprawling suburbs were home to its most destitute citizens. True to their vows, the sisters moved into a shack to live as the poor did.

A new mission in Rome joined the many others that Mother Teresa was establishing around the world. Soon, missions appeared in Tanzania, Africa; in the Aborigine territory in Australia; and in the war-torn streets of Colombo, Ceylon.

As the number of missions grew, so did the donations and the volunteers, who offered to work side by side with Mother Teresa and her sisters. One such volunteer was an Englishwoman named Anne Blaikie. She had already organized an informal group of laypeople to work with the Missionaries of Charity, but it had not been officially recognized by the pope. In 1969, Blaikie's community was officially recognized, and a new arm of the Missionaries of Charity, called the Co-Workers of Mother Teresa, was formed. Members of the Co-Workers lived and worked around the world, staying in touch with one another through an international newsletter.

Mother Teresa charged the Co-Workers with a simple task. One Co-Worker later recalled a meeting with Mother Teresa, when she told the members, "Let the Lord catch you. Let yourself be caught by Him and then let Him dispose of you utterly." Mother Teresa's admonition grew from her determination that the Co-Workers, like her missionaries, would not be fundraisers. Indeed, she insisted that Co-Workers' charitable acts begin not on the streets, but in their own homes.

She also directed them to visit residents of hospitals, nursing homes, prisons, homes for the disabled—those who had no relatives or friends to comfort them.

In 1970 the Missionaries of Charity numbered more than 1,000. With the addition of the efforts of the Co-Workers, the sisters helped the desperate in about 100 countries. Mother Teresa continued to receive awards, including, in 1971, the first Pope John XXIII Peace Prize commemorating the pope who had devoted himself to bringing peace to the world. In accepting the award, she said: "We will all make this year especially a year of peace. To this end we will try to speak more to God and with God and less to men and with men." In England, Prince Philip presented her with the 1973 Templeton Prize for Progress in Religion, an award stating in part that

*Mother Teresa kneels before Pope Paul VI in Rome and kisses the statuette of Jesus he presents to her. In awarding her the first Pope John XXIII Peace Prize, the pope said she was the symbol of brotherhood, upon which peace was based.*

"she has been instrumental in widening and deepening man's knowledge and love of God." The money and recognition Mother Teresa received allowed her to open more homes, including one in the Bronx in New York City.

As Mother Teresa's reputation grew, so did the curiosity about her. Where did this tiny bundle of energy come from? What inspired her to work so selflessly and tirelessly? Mother Teresa spoke only occasionally of her childhood, however, preferring to speak about her divine inspiration and the needs of her various missions.

She continued to be selective about her responses to the press. In the late 1960s, Malcolm Muggeridge, a director for the British Broadcasting Company, had approached Mother Teresa about producing a television program describing her work. She resisted at first, but eventually agreed on the condition that the program would be filmed in Calcutta and would show the bleak reality of her mission. Though the film crew was reportedly horrified by the sight of the sick and dying at Nirmal Hriday, they recorded it in all of its emotional detail. Called *Something Beautiful for God*, the 1969 broadcast, along with an accompanying book, attracted a great deal of attention to the various causes of the Missionaries of Charity.

Although the eyes of the world were upon her, Mother Teresa was drawn back to India in the spring of 1971. A crisis was looming in the Bengal region, in east India. The province of East Pakistan, formerly part of the republic of Pakistan, had declared its independence and taken the name Bangladesh. The new nation was Muslim, and when a civil war erupted, almost 10 million Hindu refugees fled to Bengal. Hundreds of thousands wound up on the streets of Calcutta, joining the poor who already lived in squalor. The Missionaries of Charity took on the challenge once again, offering food, medical help and, when they could, shelter.

Mother Teresa was ready to take her work one step further. She had learned through a Roman Catholic relief agency that Bangladeshi troops had raped possibly as many as 200,000 women during the conflict. Mother Teresa was determined that any women who became pregnant from the rapes would give birth to their babies. Her opposition to abortion was adamant and unchanging. With 10 other nuns, she traveled to Bangladesh in 1972 to offer help and arrange as many adoptions as possible.

Using an abandoned convent in the city of Dacca, Mother Teresa set up a home for any of the women who would seek help. She made clear her stand on abortion. "But one thing I told [the women]," she said, "was that we would take all the babies and find homes for them. Killing, I said, is killing even if the child is not yet born." In the end, not many young women went to the convent. Some did not become pregnant; others probably had abortions; for many, there was little hope. This particular rescue mission was not without controversy. The Australian feminist Germaine Greer publicly criticized the effort. A strong advocate of a woman's right to choose, Greer claimed that Mother Teresa "offered [the women] no option but to bear the offspring of hate." It was the most severe criticism Mother Teresa had received to date.

Also in 1972, Mother Teresa learned from Lazar that their mother had died in Tirana, Albania. Dranafile's dying wish had been to see her daughter once again. Age died two years later, alone in Albania. Though no doubt saddened by the losses, Mother Teresa spoke little of their deaths, simply expressing confidence that she would see her mother and her sister once again in heaven.

Mother Teresa did not allow grief to slow down her work. She was founding missions throughout the world, many in some of the most war-torn and devastated places. Those in the Middle East included homes in Jordan, the Gaza Strip, and Egypt. Another mission

*An obviously delighted Mother Teresa holds a smiling baby. Despite criticism of her adamant opposition to family planning and abortion, she remained steadfast in her conviction that every child, born or unborn, was precious and must not be allowed to die.*

was founded in Yemen, at the southwestern end of the Arabian Peninsula. After the frequent bloody skirmishes that characterized the mid-1970s Middle East conflict, the sisters tended to the wounded, the homeless, and the dying. They also arranged for as many orphans as possible to be adopted.

The Missionary Brothers of Charity had expanded as well, opening homes in Vietnam and Hong Kong. A new branch of the Missionaries of Charity, called Sisters of the Word, had also been organized. These sisters constituted a "contemplative branch" of Mother Teresa's order. Their mission was to spend all day in prayer with the exception of two hours, during which they visited the imprisoned and the sick, preaching the word of God.

Not all of Mother Teresa's missions were success stories. In 1972, when Ceylon became the nation of

Sri Lanka following a civil war, the government asked the Missionaries of Charity to leave. Plans for a mission in violence-plagued Belfast, in Northern Ireland, were quickly abandoned, probably because of threats to the sisters who would work there. Mother Teresa took such failures in stride, seeing them all as part of God's plan. In her view, as she once said, "Failure is nothing but the kiss of Jesus."

In 1975 the Missionaries of Charity celebrated the 25th anniversary of its founding. Though ill from a bad cold, Mother Teresa rose from her bed to attend mass. Sisters from five continents joined her for the thanksgiving service in Calcutta, and similar services were held at missions around the world. After the first mass of thanksgiving, Mother Teresa and her sisters attended thanksgiving services held by people of other religions. The sisters prayed in synagogues, mosques, and churches, alongside Jews, Muslims, Hindus, Buddhists, and Protestants. For Mother Teresa, it was the way to thank all who had supported her, regardless of their faith. She also wanted to demonstrate her belief that the power of prayer was universal. As she has written, "There is only one God and He is God to all; therefore it is important that everyone is seen as equal before God. I've always said we should help a Hindu become a better Hindu, a Muslim become a better Muslim, a Catholic become a better Catholic."

It was just one of the acts of kindness and reconciliation that moved people around the world.

*By 1979, Mother Teresa was a figure of international renown for her dedication to the poor, and she garnered numerous awards for her work. Here, she receives from the chairman of the Nobel Awards Committee, John Sannes, one of the world's most prestigious awards, the Nobel Peace Prize.*

# 6

# A MODEST AWARD

By 1979, much of the world was aware of Mother Teresa and her work. The Missionaries of Charity had established more than 200 facilities in some 25 nations. They were caring for thousands of the homeless and dying. Scores of their mobile clinics provided health care for thousands of patients. Their numerous schools served poor students. To most of the world's citizens, these were amazing and inspiring accomplishments.

These were the achievements that garnered Mother Teresa a nomination for the Nobel Peace Prize, one of the most prestigious international honors. She had been nominated twice in the past, but in 1979, the Nobel committee announced that she was the winner of the Peace Prize, which had been won previously by such well-known figures as Dr. Albert Schweitzer, who worked in Africa, and civil-rights activist Martin Luther King Jr. Mother Teresa was only the sixth woman to win the award.

When the news was released, the media mobbed the mission headquarters in Calcutta. Reporters and photographers filled the small parlor in the front of the house. The phone rang incessantly.

*Dressed as always in her simple white robe and sandals, Mother Teresa walks through a crowd of photographers in Oslo, Norway. Although she insisted that she was not important and that the Nobel Peace Prize was for the poor, the people of Oslo cheered her presence, greeting her with flowers, banners, and a parade.*

Telegrams of congratulations arrived from dignitaries and leaders around the world. A headline in the Calcutta newspaper *Statesman* read, "Joy Swept Calcutta."

When asked to make a statement, Mother Teresa humbly replied, "I am unworthy of the prize, but thank God for this blessed gift for the poor." True to her convictions, she did not want the glory or fame the prize would bring. Instead, she planned to use the cash award to open more facilities for lepers in India.

In December 1979, wearing her simple white sari and a sweater and coat to ward off the cold, Mother Teresa stepped from a plane at the airport in Oslo,

Norway. When a reporter approached her, she echoed what she had said earlier: "I am myself unworthy of the prize. I do not want it personally. But by this award the people of Norway have recognized the existence of the poor. It is on their behalf that I have come."

In spite of her attempt to downplay the award, the citizens of Oslo would not allow it. They decorated the streets with flowers and streamers. Pictures of Mother Teresa appeared on banners throughout the city. The awards ceremony was preceded by a torch-light procession. However, she did ask that the banquet in her honor be cancelled, and she took the money it would have cost to give to the poor.

At the ceremony, Professor John Sannes, chairman of the awards committee, explained why Mother Teresa deserved the award and the medal and the $192,000 that went with it. He reminded the audience that the year 1979 had been a year of conflicts between nations, people, and ideas. Noting the cruelty and inhumanity in the world, he went on to say it was entirely appropriate for the Nobel Committee to award the Peace Prize to Mother Teresa, who reminded people around the world to love their neighbors.

Taking her place at the podium to speak, Mother Teresa first led the international audience in the prayer of Saint Francis. Then she began her acceptance speech by telling her audience that they had been created to live God's great gift of peace. She spoke briefly about the importance of a loving family life and then launched into the primary topic of her speech—abortion.

"We are talking of peace, but, I feel that the greatest destroyer of peace today is abortion. Because it is a direct war, a direct killing—direct murder by the mother herself." She went on to say, "if a mother can kill her own child, what is left but for me to kill you and you to kill me—there is nothing in between."

What was the solution to unwanted pregnancies? In her speech, Mother Teresa insisted that adoption was the answer. She claimed that her network had placed thousands of babies in loving homes. She explained that members of the Missionaries of Charity were also teaching natural family planning—a method requiring abstinence and self-control that was approved by the Catholic Church.

The speech stirred controversy, especially in Norway, where the government funded abortions. Her words left no doubt about her stand on abortion. It was a firm conviction from which she would never waiver. She was less forthcoming about political questions. At a press conference, a reporter asked how she felt about religious persecution in Albania. She dodged the question—both its political implications and its obvious reference to her past, saying only, "My Albanian people are always in my heart."

India was anxious to celebrate its most famous citizen as well. Upon her return, Mother Teresa was honored with an official state reception. She took the opportunity to tell the story of a leper who begged on the streets of Calcutta. Hearing that Mother Teresa had won an award, he had vowed to turn over whatever he collected in his begging bowl that day to her. She placed the small amount of money he had given her on the table at the reception to show how much the tiny gift, a true gift of sacrifice, meant to her. While she kept the few coins on her table throughout the evening, she temporarily misplaced the Nobel medal she had brought to show. It was found among the coats in the entrance hall to the reception area.

A month later, the government of India awarded Mother Teresa its highest civilian honor—the Bharat Ratna, "Jewel of India." Rather than partake of the sumptuous banquet that followed the award ceremony, Mother Teresa asked if the food might be taken to her home for the dying. There, she and government officials fed an elegant meal to the patients.

In 1980 Mother Teresa was finally able to return

*Mother Teresa receives the Jewel of India, the government's highest civilian award for her work among the poor and her contribution to peace. India further honored her on her 70th birthday by putting her image on millions of postage stamps.*

home to her beloved Skopje, which was now part of Yugoslavia. While she found the town changed, she recognized the places where she had spent her happy childhood, and she was overjoyed to establish a mission there.

In addition to her awards, Mother Teresa had received honorary degrees from several universities, including secular schools as well as Catholic universities. One of the most significant degrees was a Doctor of Divinity bestowed in 1977 by Cambridge University in England. During the Protestant Reformation in the 1500s, when England broke away from the Roman Catholic Church,

*Professor John Kenneth Galbraith welcomes Mother Teresa to Harvard University, where she received an honorary Doctor of Law degree in 1982.*

Cambridge had been at the forefront of the revolt. Yet the university now honored a Catholic nun with a degree.

In 1982 Mother Teresa received an honorary Doctor of Law degree from Harvard University in Cambridge, Massachusetts. Many students at Harvard did not agree with her views on abortion but still warmly received her. The *Harvard Gazette* wrote of her: "Standing five feet tall and clad in a sarilike white habit and sandals, Mother Teresa received two standing ovations from an audience not all of whom shared her views on chastity and abortion—but clearly respected the sincerity of her appeal."

Now in demand as a speaker, Mother Teresa traveled extensively, sometimes for 10 months of the year. In her appearances, she not only encouraged people to contribute to her cause but also asked them to help the poor and destitute in their own communities. Often she walked the streets herself, visiting the poor in shelters or on the streets. She greeted whomever she met—rich or poor—with a gesture that had become her special signature. She cupped a person's head in her hands and touched her forehead to that of the other person.

In addition to her travels, Mother Teresa also extended the work of the Missionaries of Charity to include helping runaways, drug addicts, and alcoholics. She worked tirelessly and seemed to have a never-ending source of energy. In 1982, she rescued a group of disabled children in Beirut, Lebanon, who were victims of the conflict between Israelis and Palestinians. The war had raged for several years, and thousands of people had been killed and wounded.

Her official reason for going to the war-torn city was to visit the Missionaries of Charity School. Once she arrived, she learned that a group of children had been stranded in hospitals in the western part of Beirut. She was determined to cross the battle zone to rescue them, but officials refused her request. Only one other option remained for Mother Teresa—to pray for a ceasefire.

That is exactly what she and her fellow missionaries did. The very next day, a ceasefire was announced, and Mother Teresa, along with four ambulances and half a dozen Red Cross relief workers headed into the bombed-out area. There, she and her companions searched for victims, including 37 children, and took them to a safe part of the city where sisters were waiting to care for them.

"What stunned everyone," a Red Cross worker reported, "was her energy and efficiency. She saw the problem, fell

*Mother Teresa never hesitated to enter war-torn areas and rescue the victims of such conflicts. Here, she visits children in a home she founded in East Beirut, Lebanon, in 1982, during the conflict bewteen Israel and the Palestinians in that area.*

to her knees and prayed for a few seconds and then she was rattling off a list of supplies she needed."

Despite her apparent energy, Mother Teresa was beginning to show signs of her age. In 1983, in her seventies, she suffered a severe heart attack. Nevertheless, she refused to follow her doctor's advice and slow down. Indeed, she did not rest. In late 1984 the Union Carbide Company leaked poisonous gas from a chemical factory in the city of Bhopal, India. Some 3,800 died and many others were injured in one of the world's worst industrial accidents. Though the toxic fumes were still a danger, Mother Teresa immediately flew to the city where she urged the angry and distraught families of the victims to forgive those who caused the terrible tragedy. Then she immediately visited the injured in the hospital there.

In June 1985, President Ronald Reagan presented Mother Teresa with the U.S. Presidential Medal of Freedom, an award usually reserved only for Americans. President Reagan called her a "heroine of our times." She graciously accepted the medal and then responded to a request from a doctor at a Washington, D.C., hospital to visit AIDS patients.

Greeting each patient personally, Mother Teresa asked about their families and urged them to pray. She asked the doctors questions about the disease—what caused it, when the epidemic had started, and if there was a cure. She couldn't help but see parallels in the social stigma that isolated both AIDS patients and the lepers she treated in India.

While she was in Washington, Mother Teresa told an interviewer of her concern about the AIDS epidemic: "When I heard that people were dying of this terrible new disease, I knew we must do something. We care for the dying in [Nirmal Hriday], and that must be our work in New York, too. I found that the dying are mostly young men, and that some of the dying are in prison."

Mother Teresa began putting her plans for an AIDS hospice into action. On Christmas Eve of 1986 New York City mayor Edward Koch and Roman Catholic cardinal John O'Connor opened the state's first AIDS hospice in an old church in the Greenwich Village section of the city. To the media, Mother Teresa was emphatic about her goals: "We are not here to sit in judgment on these people, to decide blame or guilt. Our mission is to help them, to make their dying days more tolerable and we have sisters who are dedicated to do that."

Mother Teresa also urged New York State governor Mario Cuomo to release three prisoners in Sing Sing prison who were dying of AIDS. The governor was not immune to her pleas—and her influence. He ordered the three young men to be transferred to the hospice in Greenwich Village.

*As First Lady Nancy Reagan looks on, Mother Teresa receives the Presidential Medal of Freedom from President Ronald Reagan in 1985. While in Washington to receive the honor, she visited AIDS patients and decided to begin her plans to open hospices for AIDS victims.*

Mother Teresa and the Missionaries of Charity continued to establish hospices for AIDS victims throughout the United States. Called Gifts of Love and Gifts of Peace, centers would soon be found in Los Angeles; Washington, D.C.; and San Francisco. The Missionary Brothers of Charity also established AIDS centers, including the first day-care facility for AIDS victims in Oakland, California.

As the 1980s decade ended, Mother Teresa's frailty was noticeable. Her stooped back had worsened. She continued to suffer from heart ailments and relied on a device called a pacemaker to regulate her heart. Still, she forged ahead, focusing on establishing missions in Eastern European countries where Communist governments had begun to crumble. The situation in Romania was especially tragic. It was estimated that the turmoil in that nation had orphaned as many as 100,000 children who languished in institutions. With support of the new Romanian government, the Missionaries of Charity set up a children's home in an old sports stadium.

From Romania, Mother Teresa traveled to Czechoslovakia where she established two homes. With the success of these missions, she turned to what had become a burning passion—to establish missions in China and in Albania. Although Albania still officially banned religious practices, the government did allow Mother Teresa to establish a home in the capital, Tirana, because she claimed she intended to bring only charity to the Albanian people, not the Catholic religion.

The people of Albania welcomed Mother Teresa with open arms. She greeted those who had gathered outside the home and blessed them, proclaiming, "We have come to give tender love and care, as we do throughout the world. We will begin slowly and see what is the greatest need." She experienced a special moment of joy while visiting the graves of her mother and sister, discovering that someone unknown had been tending the graves. Mother Teresa's joy was increased when the president of Albania reversed himself and invited her to open up six previously closed churches.

At the end of 1989, Mother Teresa could take great satisfaction in her achievements. Some 40,000 people worked with the poor and sick in 92 countries. And more good news was to come. Mother Teresa and the Missionaries of Charity had finally been invited to China. But her mission to the world's most populous country would not happen for a few more years.

*Mother Teresa's legacy lives on through the dedication of the thousands of women who joined her order to carry on her work. In St. Patrick's Cathedral in New York City, she clasps the hands of a new sister as she welcomes her into the Missionaries of Charity.*

# 7

# THE LEGACY LIVES ON

In 1990, commenting about her health, Mother Teresa told a reporter: "My doctors are always telling me that I must not travel so much, that I must slow down, but I have all eternity to rest and there is so much still to do. Life is not worth living unless it is lived for others." Nevertheless, she did try to slow down as heart disease continued to plague her, and she decided that at the end of 1990 she would officially retire. Her decision charged the Missionaries of Charity with a difficult and emotional task—to find a replacement for Mother Teresa.

Who could replace Mother Teresa? After five months, the order had made no progress in finding a new leader, and Mother Teresa returned to head her order. She resumed her hectic traveling schedule—and with good humor. Once, on an Air India flight, she offered to work as a stewardess to defray the cost of the fare. Amused by her offer, airline officials gave Mother Teresa and the nuns with whom she traveled free airfare.

At the beginning of 1991, Mother Teresa became concerned about another war. The United States and its allies were fighting in the Middle East against Iraq, which had invaded and occupied the nation of Kuwait. Although she had avoided political affairs, her horror of war and its consequences impelled her to try to intervene in the Persian Gulf War. She wrote to U.S. president George Bush and Iraq's dictator, Saddam Hussein, pleading with them to "[p]lease choose the way of peace." Her letters begged the two leaders to remember that they had "the power and strength to destroy God's presence and image, his men, his women and his children. Please listen to the will of God."

The war lasted only six weeks, and massive bombing attacks by the United States and its allies destroyed much of Iraq's military and resources. Whether her letter had influenced Saddam Hussein or not, Mother Teresa was invited to go to Iraq with groups of sisters. Her mission was to offer relief to those made homeless by the war, especially the children.

Arriving in the capital city, Baghdad, on a plane chartered by the United Nations, Mother Teresa and her team were warmly greeted by government officials. They gave her a house near a hospital run by a Roman Catholic order. As pleased as she was by the welcome, she was shocked by the devastation of the war. "The fruit of war is so terrible," she noted, "one cannot understand how any human being can do that to another—and for what?" Still, she was heartened by the comfort she believed she was bringing to the people. Writing of her experience, she described her feelings: "The house is full of malnourished and crippled children. The need is so great. I do not know how long it will take to rebuild. I never thought that our presence would give so much joy to thousands of people—so much suffering everywhere."

While in Iraq, Mother Teresa found a building

suitable for a home, and she and her companions got it ready to receive the maimed and hungry children of Baghdad. She brought in teams of nuns to run the home and minister to the victims of war. The government also gave her a van so the nuns could reach out to those who could not travel to the home. A few months after her arrival, while plans were in motion for establishing other homes, Mother Teresa had to leave the country when the political situation deteriorated. The government did ask her to return when the situation had calmed down.

Mother Teresa's travels were taking a further toll on her health. In the fall of 1991, she journeyed from Calcutta to Rome and other cities in Europe. She also visited President George Bush at the White House in Washington, D.C., where she appeared particularly frail. It seemed, however, that she was consumed by a sense of urgency about what she had to accomplish. Her major purpose in visiting so many cities was to gather young women into the Missionaries of Charity.

From Washington, Mother Teresa traveled to the mission in Tijuana, Mexico. There, she contracted an especially virulent form of the flu and eventually developed bacterial pneumonia. Against her protests, she was transported to San Diego, California, where she was hospitalized. Pneumonia was not the only problem, however. Her already ailing heart was severely weakened. When news of her condition leaked out, people around the world expressed their concern. She received gracious messages from several heads of state, and the media continuously reported her condition.

Gradually Mother Teresa improved, and although still weak and hooked up to her oxygen mask, she happily took a call from Pope John Paul II. From her hospital bed she encouraged the people of San Diego to donate blood.

Finally well enough to travel, Mother Teresa headed to Rome in 1992. She visited with Anne Blaikie, one of the founders of the Co-Workers movement and a woman Mother Teresa called her "other self." Anne was seriously ill, suffering from the early stages of Alzheimer's disease—a devastating brain disorder in which the victims eventually lose control of their muscles and most of their memory. The reunion was a very emotional one for both women.

Although frail, Mother Teresa made good use of her time in Rome. Again, her work took on a kind of urgency, as if she knew she had little time left. While in the city, she arranged for the opening of a house for the Missionary of Charity Fathers.

Mother Teresa had planned on returning to Calcutta in time to meet with Great Britain's princess of Wales, Diana. The princess was herself involved in charitable work, including many of the same causes served by the Missionaries of Charity. In 1989, Mother Teresa had attended an international conference in London, where she intended to meet the princess. Due to a mix up in scheduling, that meeting never took place. Mother Teresa spoke there of the importance of Diana's work. "Everywhere there is a need for giving, and Diana has more influence over the British people than anybody else." Mother Teresa also expressed her opinion, strongly and publicly, that Princess Diana and Prince Charles should have more children. "They should be setting an example," she admonished, "sharing all their love with lots of children."

Unfortunately, Mother Teresa could not meet Diana when the princess visited Calcutta on a royal tour of India in 1992. Once again, the frail nun was hospitalized, this time in Rome. Diana did, however, visit the Missionaries of Charity. The sisters were impressed by the princess's willingness to touch and

*Diana, Princess of Wales, bends to greet Mother Teresa, who was greatly pleased by the princess's involvement in several charities. Still, Mother Teresa did not hesitate to express her views to Diana about her troubled marriage to Prince Charles.*

comfort those suffering at Nirmal Hriday.

Shortly after leaving Calcutta, Princess Diana stopped at Rome on her way home and visited Mother Teresa. Among other things, Mother Teresa tried to impress upon Diana the importance of family unity. It was no secret that Diana and Charles's marriage was in trouble, and Mother Teresa urged the young woman to pray about it. She advised that through prayer Diana and her husband could overcome their troubles and preserve their marriage.

The final breakup of Diana's marriage in 1996 disappointed Mother Teresa. In an interview, she spoke of the princess as one who was like a daughter to her. "I think it is a sad story," she said. "Diana is such a sad soul. She gives so much love but she needs to get it back."

By this time Mother Teresa's health was of concern to everyone. Her physical state could not have been helped by the fact that she and her work had come under fire on several fronts. In 1994, a program called *Hell's Angel* aired on British television, in which Mother Teresa was accused of being more interested in developing relationships with world leaders than in actually helping the poor. To make matters worse, the broadcast suggested that Mother Teresa's programs supported world leaders who were corrupt dictators. The filmmakers pointed to Mother Teresa's relationships with several such leaders, including the notorious "Baby Doc" Duvalier, dictator of Haiti, and the widow of Enver Hoxha, the much-hated Communist dictator of Albania.

As reported by an American newspaper, the *Chicago Tribune*, Mother Teresa's response to her detractors was simple and straightforward. "I reject politics completely," she said. "The poor are poor no matter if they live under a democracy or a dictatorship. In both cases they need love and care."

While many defended Mother Teresa, others used the criticism to voice similar concerns about her philosophies and her practices. The Reverend Andrew De Berry, who had met Mother Teresa years earlier in England when he was a prison chaplain, claimed that he had heard her state that the women of Calcutta should have as many children as they wanted. How many of those children, he asked, had died on the streets of India's cities?

Others questioned Mother Teresa's image as charity's superstar. A physician named Dr. Aroup Chatterjee, who was born and brought up in Calcutta, wrote a letter claiming that the image of Mother Teresa as portrayed by the media was far from her actual image in Calcutta. He claimed that many others were doing the same work as she, but they were largely ignored. He went on to suggest they were ignored because they were people of color and because they were part of a secular, not a religious, movement.

There were also others who doubted her medical practices. Mother Teresa lived by the rule that life and death were ultimately God's decision. She seemed content to let those with terminal illnesses die without the help of medication that could at least ease their pain. Many felt that the overall care at Nirmal Hriday was haphazard at best, questioning whether the patients were being diagnosed adequately. Specifically, questions arose about whether the sisters were properly distinguishing between those who were actually dying and those who could be treated. Finally, Mother Teresa's cost-savings measures were questioned. Needles and syringes were reused over and over again, increasing the risk of spreading such diseases as AIDS. Bandages and dressings were also washed and reused.

The strongest criticism of Mother Teresa and her movement had to do with the fact that their methods and philosophies were outdated and did not adequately address the underlying causes of poverty, only its effects. As one detractor pointed out, had she concentrated her efforts on a single community—Calcutta, for instance— she might have been able to raise enough funds to build a large hospital. Instead, she dispersed her funds in small amounts and her volunteer help in small groups all over the world, diluting the impact of her mission. Then, too, she continued to insist on natural birth control and to oppose abortion, and both policies had economic implications, especially in underdeveloped and developing countries.

The storm of criticism shocked Mother Teresa. She was especially distressed by the *Hell's Angel* program. "What have *they* done?" she asked. Eventually she answered the accusations by saying that she was praying for the man who spoke out against her on television. She urged her supporters to do so too. She insisted that she would not change anything. She was, she said, "living my love."

In 1993 Mother Teresa did make one change, however, and one that would stun and hurt the very people who supported her. Years earlier she had warned the congregations of Co-Workers against fund-raising. Despite her admonitions, over the years the groups received floods of money and contributions from around the world. The Co-Workers also sponsored events and distributed literature that promoted Mother Teresa's work. She had become increasingly concerned about what seemed to her a lack of simplicity and a departure from the original purpose of the Co-Workers.

Finally Mother Teresa decided to disband the organization that had served her faithfully for nearly 25 years. The news was particularly stunning in light of the support the Co-Workers had given her in the midst of the recent criticism. She gave no real reason for her decision. Perhaps some of it was motivated by the fact that her friend and original Co-Worker, Anne Blaikie, was too ill to continue her work. Undoubtedly, Mother Teresa was concerned about the funds the groups collected and the fact that the organization had become too large to manage—especially financially. There had been allegations that some funds for the poor had been diverted to the Co-Workers for travel and postage.

Whatever the reason, many of those who had served loyally at Mother Teresa's side were disappointed, although she assured them that "Co-Workers can continue to be friends with each other within a country or around the world. Friendship is a gift of God." She went on to say that their friendships should be on a private level. Although she changed her mind several times and made confusing and ambiguous statements about the organization later on, the damage she had done to some of her most ardent supporters could never be entirely undone.

Shortly after she closed down the Co-Workers, Mother Teresa suffered another blow to her health when she fell and broke three ribs while in Rome. The injury did not slow her down, however. She journeyed to Ireland, where she met campaigners against abortion and then on to London, where she once again met with Princess Diana.

In August, another round of illness landed Mother Teresa in the hospital. While in Delhi to accept an award from the Indian government, she suffered from an attack of malaria, and was striken with fever, breathlessness, and lung congestion. Her already weak heart was affected as well. She spent her 83rd birthday in the hospital recovering from another operation to open a heart vessel.

Once again, Mother Teresa survived the trauma of heart surgery. By October, she finally fulfilled her dream to bring the Missionaries of Charity to China. On the eve of the trip, Father van Exem, her dear friend and supporter of her cause, died, but not before expressing his wish that Mother Teresa establish her missions there. He told Mother Teresa that his life was an offering to God so that she and her sisters could extend their mission into China.

Mother Teresa and her entourage arrived in Shanghai, China, with an assortment of cardboard boxes to work hands-on with the poor. From Shanghai she went on to the capital, Beijing. She did not, however, set up official missions. China, she

*Frail and ailing, Mother Teresa rises from her wheelchair to speak after receiving the U.S. Congressional Medal of Honor. A fellow nun and members of Congress look on as she urges rich nations to help alleviate the plight of the world's victims of poverty.*

claimed, needed more prayer and more time. She did return to the country once again in March 1994 to establish a program for handicapped children.

Focusing on opening homes for AIDS victims, Mother Teresa tirelessly continued her travels throughout 1994 and 1995. Her work frequently brought her to the United States, where on one occasion she spoke at a prayer breakfast hosted by President Bill Clinton and First Lady Hillary Rodham Clinton. To the consternation of the listeners she made an impassioned anti-abortion speech to the group, most of whom supported legalized abortion.

In spite of the speech and the controversy it aroused in the Clinton administration, Mother Teresa became friends with Hillary Clinton. A year later, Mrs. Clinton visited one of Mother Teresa's homes in New Delhi, India. The First Lady also helped open a children's home in the Washington, D.C., area.

In 1996 Mother Teresa returned to Washington to become an honorary citizen of the United States and to receive the nation's highest honor—the Congressional Medal of Honor. Although now in a wheelchair, she rose to her feet and delivered an emotional speech about the need for rich nations, such as the United States, to serve the needs of the world's poorest citizens.

Later that year, Mother Teresa suffered her worst heart attack ever. She was too frail for additional surgery, and her condition could not be effectively treated with drugs. Mother Teresa finally insisted that the Missionaries of Charity select a new leader to take her place. She was too weak and ill to continue. She returned to her Calcutta mission and awaited their decision.

In March 1997, more than 120 delegates representing the Missionaries of Charity convened in Calcutta to elect Mother Teresa's successor. Their choice was Sister Nirmala Joshi, a 62-year-old Hindu convert to Roman Catholicism. Mother Teresa approved of the choice. Joshi, who insisted to an interviewer that she was "Sister Nirmala," not "Mother Nirmala," was one of the Missionaries of Charity's first volunteers, inspired by the work of Mother Teresa with the refugees in 1947. It was she who established the order's first mission abroad in Venezuela. Later, she became Mother Teresa's faithful companion and nurse.

One more trip was in store for Mother Teresa. Although taking oxygen three times a day, she made the journey to Rome to talk to Pope John Paul II

*The Missionaries of Charity selected Sister Nirmala Joshi as Mother Teresa's successor. Nirmala, whom one sister called a compassionate "carbon copy" of Mother Teresa, vowed to carry on her predecessor's work.*

about rehabilitating some of the city's poorer areas.

That fall, on the occasion of the death of Princess Diana in a car accident, Mother Teresa made her last public statement. She spoke fondly of the princess, recalling her devotion to the poor. She pledged to offer special prayers for Diana. On September 5, 1997, she attended mass in the morning with the other sisters. Later that afternoon, feeling pain in her chest, she refused to go to the hospital. On that evening just before the funeral of Princess Diana, her companions reported that she was standing in her room when she exclaimed, "I cannot breathe." Mother Teresa fell onto her bed, where she died. Her heart had finally ceased beating.

*Mother Teresa's death in Calcutta in September 1997 was mourned throughout India and the world. While the sisters of her order prayed around her body at their mission, India prepared a state funeral, the highest honor it could pay to the tiny nun whose selfless dedication to the poor had changed the lives of millions.*

# ANOTHER BEAUTIFUL DEATH

Mother Teresa may have been a simple woman but she would not have a simple funeral. For a short time her body lay in the chapel at the Calcutta mission so that the sisters could say good-bye. Then, an ambulance adorned with the simple word "Mother" carried her body to Calcutta's Church of St. Thomas. There, thousands upon thousands of mourners, rich and poor of all faiths, waited to pay their last respects. Clad in the familiar white sari and clasping a rosary in her hands, Mother Teresa lay under a glass dome on a platform. Some wept; others prayed. Masses of flowers, many fashioned into crosses or hearts, were left in tribute.

The Indian government announced that Mother Teresa would have a state funeral, the country's highest honor, on September 13, and flags would be flown at half-mast. On a hot and steamy day in the middle of the monsoon season, eight young army officers carried her body onto a military gun carriage that would take her to the city's large sports stadium for the official funeral. That same carriage had borne the body of

Mahandis Gandhi to his cremation. Mother Teresa's coffin, draped with the Indian national flag, was covered in white silk and festooned with wreaths and garlands of flowers.

Sister Nirmala and two other sisters of the order sat on one side of the gun carriage; several military officers sat on the other side of the carriage. Some people criticized the Indian government for allowing military soldiers to even be near Mother Teresa, a woman who had lived her life devoted to peace, and who had won the Nobel Peace Prize. For the Indian government, however, a state funeral required all the military trappings, including having soldiers guard her coffin.

Many thousands of people crowded along the streets to show their love and devotion for this tiny woman who had transformed so many lives. Some people carried banners proclaiming their love for her. Others spread flower petals along the route her carriage traveled. Many tried to break through the barriers to touch her coffin; others climbed trees and rooftops to catch a glimpse of her. One churchman who was a member of the American delegation commented, "That's where the real funeral was. In the streets."

At the transformed sports stadium, Mother Teresa's coffin was placed on a platform decorated in blue and white. The assembled viewers included some 400 of the world's most influential leaders. First Lady Hillary Rodham Clinton represented the United States. Agi Bojaxhiu, Mother Teresa's niece and only living relative, sat in a place of honor.

Thousands of invited guests filled the stands, while millions of others watched the funeral on television. Pope John Paul II, who was too ill to attend the funeral himself, sent a Vatican envoy, Cardinal Angelo Sodano, to offer a few words: "Mother Teresa of Calcutta understood fully the Gospel of love. She understood it with every fiber of her indomitable spirit and every ounce of energy in her frail body. She practiced it with her whole heart and through the daily toil of her hands."

Following the cardinal's eulogy, representatives of India's several faiths spoke of the impact Mother Teresa had had on their lives. The devout woman would have been immensely pleased to know that those she had helped so directly were a part of the service. A leper, a handicapped child, and an orphan made sacred offerings at the funeral's conclusion. Then Mother Teresa's body was carried from the stadium for a private burial, which was followed by a dramatic 21-gun salute.

While Mother Teresa was alive, many called her a "living saint." In the wake of her death, speculation arose that the pope would begin the process of declaring her an actual saint of the church. According to the laws of the Catholic Church, the canonization process cannot begin until five years after a person's death. It is a long, slow procedure. Some, like the French heroine Joan of Arc, have waited centuries to be canonized. The Catholic Church also requires that the candidate for sainthood be connected with a miracle, which generally has to occur after his or her death.

Pope John Paul II had the authority and could have bypassed the usual church requirements, but he chose not to. While Mother Teresa is not yet a saint, that could change if, at any time in the future, the pope or his successors choose to move forward with the canonization process.

Whether or not Mother Teresa becomes officially a saint, her legacy still lives on. At the time of her death, more than 4,500 Missionaries of Charity served at more than 550 centers in 126 different countries. Under the guidance of Sister Nirmala, the order is expected to grow even further and begin to address

*Nothing would have pleased Mother Teresa more than this touching poster painted by the children in Shishu Bhavan— the home she founded for them in Calcutta. Although she was a celebrity to many, her example was, as a Muslim mourner at her funeral explained simply, "a source of perpetual joy."*

MOTHER OF MANKIND

some of the underlying causes of poverty and disease.

Perhaps the strongest legacy that Mother Teresa leaves is the notion that hands-on work with the poor can truly make a difference. By simply reaching out and touching some of the most ill and destitute of the people on Calcutta's streets, Mother Teresa set an example for others to follow. By remaining humble in the face of great fame, she demonstrated that good works don't always have to be celebrated to be good. By always characterizing her work as "God's will," she showed the world the power of an abiding faith. Most of all, however, Mother Teresa touched thousands and thousands of lives—the lives of the poorest and weakest and those of the most powerful.

Mother Teresa will be remembered as one of the 20th century's most poignant symbols of peace, hope, love, and faith.

# CHRONOLOGY

1910   Agnes Gonxha Bojaxhiu born to Dranafile and Nikolas Bojaxhiu on August 26 in Skopje, Serbia

1922   Believes she has been called by God to serve the poor

1928   Enters religious order of Sisters of Loreto in Ireland; leaves as a novice to train to teach in Calcutta, India

1931   Takes first vows as a nun; adopts religious name Sister Teresa; begins teaching at St. Mary's School

1937   Takes final vows as a nun; named principal of St. Mary's School

1946   Receives a "call within a call" to serve the poor in the slums; requests permission from Pope Pius XII to work outside her convent

1948   Granted permission to work in the slums; receives some basic medical training; begins serving the poor in the streets of Calcutta

1950   Receives permission from Pope Pius XII to form a new religious order, Missionaries of Charity; leads new order as Mother Teresa; becomes a citizen of India

1952   Founds Nirmal Hriday Home for Dying Destitutes

1955   Opens home in Calcutta for abandoned children

1957   Begins working with lepers

1960   Begins establishing homes in cities throughout India; embarks on a speaking tour to the United States and Europe to publicize her missionary work

1962   Receives the Padma Shri Award for public service

1963   Helps found a brotherhood, the Missionary Brothers of Charity

1965   Receives permission from Pope Paul VI to expand her work outside India; sets up first international home in Cocorote, Venezuela

1968   Establishes mission in Rome, Italy, at the request of Pope Paul VI

1969   Accepts a new arm of the Missionaries of Charity, the Co-Workers, comprised of lay volunteers around the world

1971   Receives the first Pope John XXIII Peace Prize

1972   Travels to war-torn Bangladesh to arrange adoptions of unwanted children; receives Jawaharlal Nehru Award for International Understanding

1973   Becomes the first recipient of Britain's Templeton Prize for Progress in Religion

1979    Awarded the Nobel Peace Prize

1980    Receives India's Bharat Ratna ("Jewel of India") Award; returns for the first time to her birthplace, Skopje, now part of Yugoslavia

1982    Visits Missionaries of Charity missions in war-torn Lebanon to help rescue disabled children; begins speaking tour of the United States; awarded honorary Doctor of Law degree by Harvard University

1983    Suffers a severe heart attack

1985    Presented with U.S. Presidential Medal of Freedom by President Ronald Reagan; begins plans to open hospices for AIDS victims

1990    Announces plans to retire as leader of Missionaries of Charity; remains as head of order when no replacement is found

1991    Travels to Baghdad, Iraq, following the Gulf War to set up homes for war victims; visits cities in Europe; travels to mission in Tijuana, Mexico; falls ill and is hospitalized

1992    Meets Diana, Princess of Wales, in Rome

1993    Disbands the Co-Workers; makes her first trip to China

1994    Is criticized for her ideas and relationships with world leaders; establishes a program for handicapped children in China

1996    Receives honorary U.S. citizenship; awarded the U.S. Congressional Medal of honor; resigns as head of the Missionaries of Charity

1997    Successor is chosen; Mother Teresa dies of heart failure on September 5; receives state funeral from government of India

# BIBLIOGRAPHY

Allegri, Renzo. *Teresa of the Poor: The Life of Mother Teresa of Calcutta.* Ann Arbor, Mich.: Servant Publications, 1998.

"Ballantine Sets Mother Teresa Book for October." *Publishers Weekly,* 17 July 1995.

Brown, Ray B., ed. *Contemporary Heroes and Heroines, Book I.* Gale Research, 1990.

Chawla, Navin. *Mother Teresa: The Authorized Biography.* Rockport, Mass.: Element Books, 1996.

Clinton, William. *The Presidential Radio Address.* Weekly Compilation of Presidential Documents, September 5, 1997.

Devardi, Brother Angelo, ed. *Total Surrender: Mother Teresa.* New York: Walker and Company, 1993.

Doig, Desmond. *Mother Teresa: Her People and Her Work.* New York: Harper & Row, 1976.

Egan, Eileen M. *Such a Vision of the Street.* Garden City, N.Y.: Doubleday, 1985.

_____. "Blessed Are the Merciful: Mother Teresa (1910–1997)." *America,* 20 September 1997.

"For the Poor, an Immortal." *Time,* 22 September 1997.

Frankel, Bruce, and Jan McGirk. "The Last Goodbye." *People Weekly,* 29 September 1997.

Gates, David. "Trashing Mother Teresa." *Newsweek,* 13 November 1995.

Lee, Betsy. *Mother Teresa: Caring for All God's Children.* Minneapolis, Minn.: Dillon, 1981.

LeJoly, Edward S.J. *Mother Teresa of Calcutta.* San Francisco: Harper & Row, 1985.

"Living Saints: Messengers of Love and Peace." *Time,* 29 December 1975.

Mitchell, Emily, et al. "Saint of the Streets." *People Weekly,* 22 September 1997.

"Mother Teresa, 1910–1997," *Biography Today,* April 1998.

"Mother Teresa." *Encyclopedia of World Biography,* 2nd ed. Gale Research, 1998.

"Mother Teresa." *Newsmakers 1998.* Gale Group, 1998.

"Mother Teresa Buried in Calcutta." *Christian Century*, 24 September 1997.

"Mother Teresa in New York to Initiate Nuns into Order." *New York Times*, 27 May 1997.

"Mother Teresa's Mourners Throng to Grieving Calcutta." *New York Times*, 7 September 1997.

"Mother Teresa's Order Chooses a New Leader." *New York Times*, 14 March 1997.

Pond, Mildred M. *Mother Teresa: A Life of Charity*. Philadelphia: Chelsea House Publishers, 1992.

Ruth, Amy. *Mother Teresa*. Minneapolis, Minn.: Lerner, 1999.

Sebba, Anne. *Mother Teresa: Beyond the Image*. New York: Doubleday, 1997.

Spink, Kathryn. *Mother Teresa*. San Francisco: HarperCollins, 1997.

Thornton, Jeannye. "St. Teresa of Calcutta." *US News and World Report*, 22 September 1997.

Walljasper, Jay. "Christopher Hitchens Versus Mother Teresa." *Utne Reader*, July/August, 1995.

Wellman, Sam. *Mother Teresa: Missionary of Charity*. Philadelphia: Chelsea House Publishers, 1999.

Woodward, Kenneth. "Requiem for a Saint." *New York Times*, 22 September, 1997.

# INDEX

# INDEX

# PICTURE CREDITS

**Tracey E. Dils** is the author of more than 25 books for young readers, including *Annabelle's Awful Waffle; What I Do, the Monster Does Too; Grandpa's Magic; Real Life Scary Places; Real Life Strange Encounters;* and *A Look around Coral Reefs*. Her book *A Young Author's Guide to Publishers* received the Parent's Choice Award for 1997. Tracey is also the recipient of the prestigious Ohioana Award in Children's Literature for her contribution to the field. When Tracey isn't writing, she works at an educational publishing company as an executive editor. Tracey is also a frequent speaker at writers' conferences for both children and adults across the country. She lives in Columbus, Ohio, with her husband, Richard, and her children, Emily and Phillip.

**Matina S. Horner** was president of Radcliffe College and associate professor of psychology and social relations at Harvard University. She is best known for her studies of women's motivation, achievement, and personality development. Dr. Horner has served on several national boards and advisory councils, including those of the National Science Foundation, Time Inc., and the Women's Research and Education Institute. She earned her B.A. from Bryn Mawr College and her Ph.D. from the University of Michigan, and holds honorary degrees from many colleges and universities, including Mount Holyoke, Smith, Tufts, and the University of Pennsylvania.